UNICEF INNOCENTI RESEARCH CENTRE

The UNICEF Innocenti Research Centre in Florence, Italy, was established in 1988 to strengthen the research capability of the United Nations Children's Fund (UNICEF) and to support its advocacy for children worldwide. The Centre (formally known as the International Child Development Centre) helps to identify and research current and future areas of UNICEF's work. Its prime objectives are to improve international understanding of issues relating to children's rights and to help facilitate the full implementation of the United Nations Convention on the Rights of the Child in both industrialized and developing countries.

The Centre's publications are contributions to a global debate on child rights issues and include a wide range of opinions. For that reason, the Centre may produce publications that do not necessarily reflect UNICEF policies or approaches on some topics. The views expressed are those of the authors and are published by the Centre in order to stimulate further dialogue on child rights.

The Centre collaborates with its host institution in Florence, the Istituto degli Innocenti, in selected areas of work. Core funding for the Centre is provided by the Government of Italy, while financial support for specific projects is also provided by other governments, international institutions and private sources, including UNICEF National Committees.

Contents

UNICEF
Innocenti Insight

THE TWO FACES OF EDUCATION IN ETHNIC CONFLICT

Towards a Peacebuilding Education for Children

WITHDRÁWN

Edited by
Kenneth D. Bush
Diana Saltarelli

dren's Fund
Centre

ACKNOWLEDGEMENTS

This study draws on the findings of a project originated and coordinated by Paolo Basurto, former director of the UNICEF International Child Development Centre (now known as the UNICEF Innocenti Research Centre). The editorial team wishes to thank all those who assisted in the preparation of this publication. For contributions to the main text: Sami Adwan, Paulo Basurto, Kenneth D. Bush, Aziz Esmail, Robert Ferguson, Ruth Firer, Anthony M. Gallagher, Jagdish Gundara, Stephen P. Heyneman, Peter Newell, and Diana Saltarelli. For assistance in initiating the project and in carrying out research: Paola Sanchez-Moreno. For reviewing background papers and providing guidance on the scope of the current study, in addition to the main contributors, Alan Phillips of Minority Rights Groups International, London. For coordinating the project's research in Israel and Gaza and the West Bank, Marilena Viviani, Special Representative, UNICEF Jerusalem; and for his support of this work, Gamini Abeysekera, Representative, UNICEF Bangkok, Thailand, formerly Special Representative, UNICEF Jerusalem.

Kenneth D. Bush is Research Fellow at Dalhousie University, Canada.
Diana Saltarelli is a Research Consultant and Editor on human rights issues.

Cover design: Miller, Craig & Cocking, Oxfordshire - UK
Layout and phototypesetting: Bernard & Co, Siena - Italy
Printed by Arti Grafiche Ticci, Siena - Italy

ISBN 88-85401-67-8

August 2000

Front cover picture: © UNICEF/HQ97-0583/Roger Lemoyne
A map of Albania on the blackboard behind her, a girl stands in a classroom in the northern city of Shkodra, addressing classmates during a UNICEF-assisted psychosocial rehabilitation programme to help children cope with the effects of recent civil unrest.

Foreword

The *Two Faces of Education in Ethnic Conflict* challenges a widely-held assumption – that education is inevitably a force for good. While the provision of good quality education can be a stabilizing factor, Kenneth Bush and Diana Saltarelli show how educational systems can be manipulated to drive a wedge between people, rather than drawing them closer together. In short, education reflects the society around it. The attitudes that flourish beyond the school walls will, inevitably, filter into the classroom.

The report begins by describing the nature of today's armed conflicts, with virtually every conflict of recent years fought within, rather than between, nations. It examines the growing importance of 'ethnicity' in conflicts, as clearly seen in recent tragedies such as Rwanda, Kosovo and Chechnya.

Section two describes the two very different faces of education. The negative face shows itself in the uneven distribution of education to create or preserve privilege, the use of education as a weapon of cultural repression, and the production or doctoring of textbooks to promote intolerance. The positive face goes beyond the provision of education for peace programmes, reflecting the cumulative benefits of the provision of good quality education. These include the conflict-dampening impact of educational opportunity, the promotion of linguistic tolerance, the nurturing of ethnic tolerance, and the 'disarming' of history.

While Bush and Saltarelli recognize the value of peace education, they stress that it is only one of many educational measures needed in the midst of ethnic hatred. Curriculum packages that promote tolerance will have little impact if they are delivered within educational structures that are fundamentally intolerant. Peace education cannot succeed without measures to tackle the destructive educational practices that fuel hostility, and should be seen as one part of a wider peacebuilding education approach. Peacebuilding education is a process rather than a product, long-term rather than short-term, relying on local, rather than external, inputs and resources, seeking to create opportunities rather than impose solutions

Peacebuilding education goes further than the 'add good education and stir' approach, aiming to transform the very foundations of intolerance. Sadly, these foundations are controlled by the same political or ideological forces that control education, making the necessary transformation immensely difficult. Such change would threaten the structures of authority, dominance and control – in the North as well as the South.

The study examines possible steps towards the creation of a peacebuilding education, outlining guiding principles and goals, including the demilitarization of the mind, the introduction of alternatives to suspicion, hatred and violence, and the value of memory.

The Two Faces of Education has been prepared with the support of the UNICEF Innocenti Research Centre in Florence, Italy, which is committed to researching new areas that affect the implementation of the Convention on the Rights of the Child.

Mehr Khan
Director
UNICEF Innocenti Research Centre

Introduction

This study seeks to develop a clearer understanding of one particular dimension of contemporary ethnic conflict: the *constructive* and *destructive* impacts of education – the two faces of education. The need for such analysis is apparent from even a cursory review of experiences in conflict-prone regions. Because educational initiatives can have polar opposite impacts, those involved must stop supporting peace-destroying educational initiatives, and start supporting those aimed at peacebuilding. In other words, if such educational initiatives are to have a positive peacebuilding impact, then they must seek to *deconstruct structures of violence and construct structures of peace*. The ways in which this might be achieved are addressed in the final section of this study.

Most of the world's armed conflicts are civil wars. Of the 25 armed conflicts in 1997, only one – between India and Pakistan – was interstate. All the others were internal conflicts. (SIPRI Yearbook 1998, Oxford University Press, 1999). The current trend is to label these conflicts 'ethnic', perhaps to distinguish them from the conflicts of the past, when the underlying problems seemed to be ideological and political. Now they appear at first glance to be motivated by the fact of one's religion, traditions, the colour of one's skin or any other reason that is not openly ideological or economic in nature.

Countries that have endured such conflicts have diverted vast amounts of resources, both economic and human, to support military actions. 'Victory', if ever finally declared, has a very hollow ring indeed. In such conflicts there are no victors, only victims. Such countries often find themselves in a state of complete economic and social collapse. In the aftermath of the 1994 Rwanda genocide – which resulted in the deaths of an estimated 800,000 children, women and men – the national economy was decimated, and almost every institution of local and central government destroyed. Large portions of international aid that could have gone to development were, instead, diverted to emergency assistance. It is estimated that international emergency relief to Rwandan refugees and displaced persons during nine months in 1996 alone amounted to US$ 1.4 billion (Sellstrom and Wohlgemuth, 1996; Cantwell, 1997).

The structures and processes that appear to turn ethnic intolerance into unbridled violence are highly complex. A list of causal factors might include 'historical forces', economic tensions, 'bad' governance, perceived threats to cultural identity and (in ways that are not adequately understood) formal, non-formal and informal educational processes. Ethnicity itself is often asserted to be a key contributor to 'ethnic conflict'. However, it is increasingly evident that "ethnicity neither causes conflict, nor in many cases does it accurately describe it. Rather ethnicity/identity is increasingly mobilized and politicized in contemporary violent conflicts" (Bush, 1997).

There are many theories attempting to explain the formation of ethnic identity and some are introduced below. However, this study focuses on the educational structures and processes that politicize identities in ways that allow diversity and cultural difference to become the basis for violent, protracted, conflict. Historically, much attention has been paid to 'racial' differences, but this has tended to obscure some of the underpinning dynamics of the problem. Today, we are quite aware that race is a social and political construction, a social fact – or fiction, if you will – with no biological basis. Nonetheless, such differences have been used – and continue to be used – as a pretext for treating people differently. The reality is that any difference, however accidental or barely perceptible, may be used as a pretext for discriminatory practices.

The impact of violent ethnic conflicts on children is profound. According to the 1996 United Nations report on the *Impact of Armed Conflict on Children*, coordinated by Graça Machel[1], two million children died during armed conflicts between 1986 and 1996. Six million children were seriously injured or permanently disabled, and millions more were separated from their families, physically abused, abducted into military groups and, particularly in the case of girls, traumatized by sexual violence and rape. In Rwanda alone, as many as 300,000 children were killed within a period of three months in 1994, while vast numbers were physically and psychologically maimed and forced to flee their homes (Cantwell, 1997). In Chechnya, 40 per cent of civilian casualties from February to May 1995 were children (UN, 1996a). In Bosnia and Herzegovina, over 15,000 children were killed during fighting. Classrooms had to move underground to protect children from snipers (UNICEF Yugoslavia, 1994).

James Wolfenson, President of the World Bank, once observed that 'true' development could be distinguished from fake development by "the smile on the face of a child". The importance of this very human and basic observation should not be underestimated. It sees the well-being of children as the essential measure of all development and peace work. The well-being of children, rather than abstract and complex indicators, becomes the most immediate and transparent measure of the well-being of an entire community. While there are challenges to collecting this type of information, it is an especially important and sensitive means of measuring and assessing conditions in conflict-prone settings because it focuses on those who are typically the first and most directly affected populations – children and women. Given the large number of conflicts still raging today, their devastating consequences and enormous costs, it becomes essential to ask not just how the damage can be repaired, but more importantly how future conflicts can be prevented or at least foreseen.

Our current state of knowledge about the specific mechanisms that generate armed conflicts is expressed well by James Rule (1988) when he writes, "We know a lot of things that are true about civil violence, but we do not know when they are going to be true."

Education on its own can not be expected to manage or resolve identity-based violent conflicts, just as diplomatic and peacekeeping initiatives on their own cannot be expected to resolve militarized conflict in the absence of complementary political, economic and social initiatives. Any solution to violent conflict will be sustainable only if it is developed and supported by both governmental and non-governmental actors within violence-affected societies in ways that are consistent with the fundamental and universal principles of human rights.

---

1 - United Nations, 1996a. 'Impact of Armed Conflict on Children', Graça Machel.

The UNICEF Innocenti Research Centre Study

This Study is an expression of UNICEF's commitment to work for the protection of children's rights, within the framework of the Convention on the Rights of the Child. The UNICEF Innocenti Research Centre (IRC) helps to identify and research emerging areas that may affect the implementation of the Convention. The profound change in the nature of warfare over recent decades is an obvious example, as it has had a major impact on children. They are increasingly targeted for violence on the basis of their 'ethnic' identity.

Many factors contribute to peaceful or conflict-ridden coexistence between different ethnic groups within a society, but it is clear to many observers that education plays a definite role. The central objective of the study is to gain a better understanding of the nature of the many linkages between three key areas - education, ethnicity and conflict.

The study began life as a small research project carried out in 1997-1998 at UNICEF IRC (then known at the International Child Development Centre). A group of experts was appointed to define how best to analyze the connections between ethnicity, education and conflict, to advise on data collection and analysis, prepare relevant questionnaires and suggest suitable research participants. A network was created among institutions and individuals already working in the three key areas, serving as a source of information for the study and as a 'sounding board' for its ideas.

Since education can have either a socially destructive or constructive impact, it is useful to examine the educational experiences within and between a wide spectrum of countries, including those *not* caught up in ethnicized conflicts as well as those that are. The studies were carried out in 1997-98.

The guiding question for this work was when, why, and how does education affect ethnic conflict – positively and negatively. For the purpose of this Study, education was broadly defined as an important medium for imparting not only pedagogic instruction but attitudes, values and behaviours (Black, 1996). It transmits language, culture, moral values and social organization, leading to a particular identity and often has a strong political role. It is understood to rest on two distinct foundations:
- the *formal structures* of schooling (a teacher who teaches and a student who learns)
- the *informal and non-formal structures* of learning – involving the acquisition of ideas, values, beliefs and opinions outside educational institutions, whether in streets, fields, religious settings or the home.

Informal education is learning that occurs without being specifically planned and structured. Examples might be socialization, learning how to behave in a family or learning a trade from a parent. Non-formal education is planned and organized, offering specific learning environments and opportunities. These are usually more flexible and open than the formal education typified by schooling.

The project began with the observation that formal education is often viewed as a neutral or technical process of information dissemination set within a given societal context. It found that this starting point inhibited consideration of the role of education in the creation of a "constructed" – rather than a "given" – societal context. The broadening of the analytical focus reveals that implicitly and explicitly, intentionally and unintentionally, education *inevitably* has a societal impact – for good or for ill. As the author and critic Neil Postman has said,

"... public education does not serve a public. It creates a public. The question is, what kind of public does it create? A conglomerate of self-indulgent consumers? Angry, soulless, directionless masses? Indifferent, confused citizens? Or a public imbued with confidence, a sense of purpose, a respect for learning and tolerance?" (Postman 1996, p.18).

The approach adopted in this Study is interdisciplinary. It attempts to integrate contributions from different communities and to establish a set of common understandings that might help to focus analytical and policy efforts. This makes sense both conceptually and practically: complex and multi-dimensional problems must be matched with multifaceted responses.

The study draws a clear distinction between violent and non-violent conflict. It does not see the latter as a necessarily negative or destructive phenomenon. Development, for example, is *inevitably* conflictual, destabilizing, or subversive because it challenges the established power structures that prevent individuals and groups from reaching their full potential. While the study focuses more on violent, than on non-violent conflict, it has a special interest in those moments when a conflict tips over the edge into actual violence. At such moments, the presence or absence of conflict-mediating mechanisms and institutions may determine whether a conflict crosses that threshold. These may include representative political systems, a transparent and fair judicial system, or an equitable social system.

While the study has a particular interest in education systems, it attempts to understand these within the broader political, economic, and social institutional context. Some have argued that violent conflict is the ultimate expression of the breakdown of a society's governance system, and that reconstruction therefore rests primarily upon the renegotiation and refashioning of new systems of governance at the community, sub-national and national level. Thus, 'reconstruction' requires strategies and interventions to promote institutional arrangements that can facilitate and sustain the transition from violent conflict to sustainable development, and build 'fire walls' that prevent societal conflict spiralling into societal violence. An appealing feature of the study's broad approach is the way analysis of the problems is tied to an understanding of solutions.

This study should be considered as a first attempt to explore a set of highly complex and controversial issues. Its potential contribution is twofold: a focused and critical examination of the peace-building *and peace-destroying* role of education; and the placement of children on the mainstream peace-building and reconstruction agenda in a way that goes beyond their necessary but narrow inclusion as child soldiers.

1. THE CONTEMPORARY IMPORTANCE OF ETHNICITY

■ 1.1 A REVIEW OF PERSPECTIVES ON ETHNICITY

As ethnicity has re-emerged as a key dimension in public affairs within and between States, we have seen a rise in awareness of the importance of ethnic issues within social theory. While social theorists in the 19th and early 20th centuries were interested in conflict in society, the theoretical flavour of the mid-20th century tended to neglect conflict in favour of a unitary notion of society and culture. This approach emphasized social integration through common values. Conflict was seen as pathological and dysfunctional to the normal operations of society. More recently, non-violent social conflict has been seen to contain the potential for a positive role in producing the processes and structures of group cohesion by creating a sense of unity that cross-cuts individual identity (Darby, 1991).

In another area of social theory, social stratification, there has been a recent recognition of the need to incorporate ethnic stratification alongside the more traditional dimensions of investigation such as gender and socio-economic stratification (Parkin, 1979). In a key text in the literature on ethnicity, Glazer and Moynihan (1975) reversed a long tradition within social theory to argue that ethnicity had become the fundamental basis of social stratification in contemporary society, with property now appearing to be derivative. By the early 1990s the literature on ethnic issues and ethnicity had grown considerably. A key feature of this literature has been a break with the 'modernization' paradigm, which had predicted that the processes of urbanization, secularization and industrialization would minimize social differences, while nation-building would develop modern homogeneous culture centred around patriotic loyalty to the state, rather than to ethnically based loyalties such as nationalism. The supposed promise of the modernization paradigm was that "ascriptive group loyalties would be superseded and would no longer be functional in modern societies", but this promise proved illusory (Bacal, 1991).

The renewed attention to ethnicity can be seen across academic disciplines. Social anthropologists were among the first social scientists to address issues of ethnicity in studies of isolated and distant cultures (Rex, 1986). Social psychologists have long been interested in the dynamics of prejudice and discrimination, but for the present purposes what is perhaps even more significant is the shift, over the last 20 years, in European social psychology towards intergroup research and theory, and a focus on the processes of social identity (Tajfel, 1984). There is a further point of contact between historical, sociological and psychological research on genocide and ethnocide (Baumann, 1989; Chalk and Jonassohn, 1990; Staub, 1989).

Political scientists have offered ideas on the role of electoral and governmental systems in plural societies (De Guchtenere et al, 1991), while the discipline of international relations has made an important contribution to issues of governance at national and international levels, and to conflict resolution through mediation (Groom, 1991). More specifically, there have been some outstanding contributions to the politics of ethnicity that have analyzed, among other issues: the nature and origins of ethnic affiliations; the material sources of identity-based conflict; ethnicity and party politics;

ethnicized military structures; and inter-ethnic accommodation – in short, the logic and structure of ethnic conflict and on measures to abate it (Horowitz 1985; Esman 1994; Montville 1989; Brass 1991; Connor 1994).

Educationalists have long been interested in ethnic and racial issues, in terms of the participation of ethnic minorities in educational systems, the potential role of education in ameliorating discrimination (Coulby et al., 1997; Pluralism in Education, 1996) and the importance of these issues for teacher training (Craft, 1996; Martinez, 1994). While these issues have been most extensively addressed in Western states, there has been a broader, comparative interest in education and human rights (Grant, 1988; Kymlicka, 1996; Tarrow, 1987; Modgil et al, 1986). The area of human rights and minority rights has inspired a huge literature with a strong focus on the international legal framework (Davies, 1988).

The key point arising from this review of the literature is that the study of ethnicity and conflict is not the exclusive purview of any single academic discipline or school. Rather, the study of ethnicity marks a point of intersection that has attracted the attention of many schools of thought.

Drawing on this vast literature, this study understands ethnicity to be a form of cultural distinctiveness. This implies that the idea of an ethnic group only makes sense in the context of ethnic pluralism. Ethnic identity may evolve gradually, or be imposed – or some combination of the two. At a voluntaristic level, an ethnic group is a community of people who engage in shared social practices that reinforce their sense of identity: examples would include religious, linguistic and cultural communities. A useful point of departure is the definition by the academic Paul Brass: "*ethnicity* is the subjective, symbolic, or emblematic use by a group of people of any aspect of culture in order to create internal cohesion and differentiate themselves from other groups."[2] This understanding of ethnicity recognizes that the internal and external functions of group identity are cohesion and differentiation. Central to this sense of identity is a shared belief in common descent, birth or

kinship, which may be (but usually is not) based on biological fact. Stavenhagen defines ethnic groups as collectivities that have both objective and subjective characteristics. Their members acknowledge sharing common traits such as language, culture or religion, as well as a sense of belonging.

Ethnic identity may be based also on assumed national origins, or on shared phenotypic characteristics such as skin colour. In either case, the basis for ethnic affiliation establishes a particular community as distinctive and bounded in some way or other. This distinctiveness should not be seen as unalterable or immutable. The multiplicity of available identities only becomes of social and political relevance when a particular basis for identity is invested with social meaning and significance. This implies that ethnicity, and the notion of an ethnic group, does not exist in any abstract sense, but is always linked to a particular place and a particular time. At a theoretical and conceptual level, therefore, ethnic boundaries are socially constructed and hence malleable, even though in particular contexts they may be treated as timeless and unalterable. The labelling of members of ethnic groups along stereotypical lines, for example, is usually linked to the maintenance of a power imbalance between the minority (or minorities) and an ethnic majority.

It is, however, important to recognize and emphasize the positive, integrating force of ethnicity in contemporary societies. While most, if not all, societies are ethnically plural, not all suffer violent internal conflict between ethnic communities. There is value in assessing social policy and practice in societies that have flourished through the celebration of pluralism and diversity.

■ 1.2 CHILDREN'S ETHNIC SOCIALIZATION

The processes and structures that influence and shape ethnic attitudes in children are still not agreed upon despite considerable research.

---

2 - Paul Brass, *Ethnicity and Nationalism: Theory and Comparison* (New Delhi: Sage, 1991), p. 19.

However, within the context of ethnic conflict, the importance of developing a better understanding of this dynamic is underscored by the finding by Padilla, Ruiz and Brand (1974) that ethnic attitudes are formed early, and that once positive or negative prejudices are formed, they tend to increase with time. Early socialization experiences are, therefore, critical in the formation of ethnic attitudes. There are many components that make up these experiences for each child. In the broadest sense, Riegel (1976) argues that socio-cultural attitudes and identities are a function of the interaction of historical socio-cultural milieu, individual factors and the physical environment. Together, these are understood to form unique patterns of development for each generation, each ethnic group and each individual. While the generalization of this finding limits its use in understanding the specific instances and cases of ethnic socialization and conflict, there are a number of avenues of inquiry that are more directly applicable to the current study.

Researchers within the psychoanalytic tradition tend to focus on personality types. They see negative attitudes as being determined by early childhood experience, especially parent-child relationships. This suggests that education will have to target both children and parents if it is to play a constructive role in inter-ethnic relations. It also suggests that the impact of formal schooling programmes will be tempered by the influence of extra-curricular inputs. In other words, the boundary between school and society is permeable – particularly in the area of ethnic socialization.

Children do not come to the classroom as blank slates. They bring with them the attitudes, values and behaviour of their societies beyond the classroom walls. In this context, even the early research in contemporary social sciences indicates that children who show less acceptance of other groups tend to be more constricted, cynical, suspicious and less secure than children who are more tolerant (Adorno, Frenkel-Brunswick, Levinson and Sanford 1950). Prejudiced children are more likely to be moralistic, to dichotomize the world, to externalize conflict, and to have a high need for definiteness (Allport 1954). Under conditions of inter-ethnic tension and conflict, such characteristics unavoidably find their way into

Altering the rules of ethnic interaction

A central question for the current study is the degree to which, and the conditions under which, education can play a constructive role – not necessarily in altering the content of group identities but in altering the rules of ethnic interaction.

In this way, formal schooling and training, as well as non-formal education, can play an essential role in conflict transformation, whether to sensitize a society to inequities in a system; to foster tolerance and inter-group understanding; to promote healing and reconciliation; or to nurture the idea and capacities for peace. These are challenges currently being addressed in a number of places including Mozambique, Northern Ireland and South Africa.

When social psychologists shift the analytical focus to group processes that influence and shape prejudicial attitudes and cross-ethnic attitudes, a variety of factors emerge, including proximity, frequency of contact, ethnic balance, density, heterogeneity of the population and the degree of vertical mobility within society (Le Vine and Campbell 1972). Only gradually through direct contact, and increasingly via the media, do children learn that some of their behaviour, which to them is the only way to behave in a given situation, is, in fact, 'ethnic'. While children may become aware of the more obvious ethnic clues, such as language and skin colour, at a very early age, they may not realize that they think and behave differently in certain situations to individuals from other ethnic groups until adulthood (if then). In integrated school settings, children may be exposed to other groups and their different characteristics. This awareness of difference opens the door to conscious choice: to emphasize one's own distinctive patterns, to adopt the patterns of the other group, or to fashion a middle ground of inter-cultural accommodation.

the classroom and must thus be taken into account if the peace-destroying impact of education is to be minimized. In Sri Lanka, for example, the ethnic chauvinism and stereotyping that are rampant outside the classroom find their way into the classroom through textbooks used in social studies classes (within both majority and minority communities). This exacerbates an inter-connected and socially corrosive dynamic inside and outside school walls. However, if the border between schooling and society is indeed permeable, this opens up the possibility that students may carry non-confrontational and tolerant attitudes from the classroom into the broader community. Just as teachers may be role models to the students they teach, so students may play an active role in shaping the attitudinal and perceptual environment beyond the walls of the school.

In Bosnia, when buses filled with women in the final months of pregnancy from rape were sent back across enemy lines covered with vicious graffiti about the children about to be born, there could be no doubt that the violence was intended to be both individual and collective.

■ 1.3 THE NEW MATH OF ETHNIC VIOLENCE

Statistics sketch a general picture of the changing situation. In the late 1970s, 18 states had significant internal linguistic conflicts and 19 had significant internal religious conflicts. In 1983, 76 States had active opposition groups organized around minority grievances, while a further 38 had evidence of minority grievances, but no organized opposition groups. In as many as 41 States, minority opposition groups used violent methods to press their claims (Kidron and Segal, 1984). More recent data serve to reinforce this picture. In 1996 Darby (1997) estimated that there were 74 active violent political conflicts, 19 of which had resulted in more than 1,000 deaths in that single year. The annual yearbooks of the Stockholm Peace Research Institute (SIPRI) suggest that, throughout the 1990s, there were about 30 active major armed conflicts, only one of which was interstate. The rest took place within States, between factions split along ethnic, religious or cultural lines.[3]

While some internal conflicts have been contained, many have intensified, including those in the countries of the former Yugoslavia, Nagorno-Karabakh, the Kurdish regions of Eastern Turkey, the Horn of Africa, Rwanda, Lebanon, in Sri Lanka and a number of flashpoints in the Indian sub-continent. Many have assumed international dimensions. Indeed, few ethnic minorities are confined to a single State. Ethnic identity often ignores national borders. There are Serbs in Croatia and Bosnia, Russians within many of the successor states of the USSR, and Kurds and Chinese in many Asian countries. It is not surprising, therefore, that ethnic minority groups often look to neighbouring countries for protection or occasionally make irredentist claims.

■ 1.4 NATURE AND DYNAMICS OF VIOLENT ETHNIC CONFLICT

Contemporary violent conflicts – especially ethnic conflicts – are increasingly dirty. From Algeria to Omagh to Sri Lanka, the principal weapon of war is terror. Not only do warriors target civilians, and especially children, systematically,[4] but they employ control through the creation and manipulation of fear.[5] Their strategies include scorched earth tactics to starve populations and destroy infrastructures, sexual torture and mass rape, ethnic and social cleansing, and even genocide.

Once violence becomes fuelled by hyper-politicized identity, an insidious logic kicks in

---

3 - UN, 1996a, op. cit.

4 - Some analysts have estimated that the civilian casualty rate in today's conflicts are around 90% compared with 50% in World War I and 66% in World War II. Christer Ahlstrom, *Casualties of Conflict: Report for the World Campaign for the Victims of War.* Department of Peace and Conflict Research, 1991.

5 - For clear discussions of the use of terror as a weapon of dirty war, see: Carolyn Nordstrom, Backyard Front, in Nordstrom and JoAnn Martin, eds., *The Paths to Domination, Resistence and Terror.* University of California Press, 1992; and Juan E. Corradi, Patricia Weiss Fagen and Manuel Antonio Garreton, eds., *Fear at the Edge: State Terror and Resistance in Latin America* (University of California Press, 1992).

that raises the stakes beyond the more negotiable issues such as territorial control or the redistribution of political and material resources. In identity-based conflicts, the very existence of a community is thought to be under threat. An opposing identity group is labelled as the source of the threat and the battlefield expands to include homes and playgrounds. An individual comes to be targeted *because* of his or her membership in a particular community. The physical, psychological and moral violence inflicted on individuals is meant to affect the community as a whole – specifically, the identity group of which that individual is a member.

However abhorrent contemporary manifestations of ethnicized violence may be, their systematic and institutionalized character suggests an underpinning instrumentalist logic – whether it is territorial control through ethnic cleansing, or direct attacks on the morale and cultural fabric of a community through mass rape. The element of spectacle becomes essential for meeting strategic military and political objectives and the very bodies of individuals become a public battleground. In Bosnia, when buses filled with women in the final months of pregnancy from rape were sent back across enemy lines covered with vicious graffiti about the children about to be born, there could be no doubt that the violence was intended to be both individual and collective. As intended, these women continue to be victimized after their return by being ostracized by their communities – a further fragmentation of a community.

A kill-or-be-killed logic requires, and justifies, war against both immediate *and future* threats. When the language of future threats is combined with dehumanization, demonization, and zero-sum logic, then children and women become threats to be eliminated – from the gas chambers of Nazi Germany, to the killing fields of Pol Pot's Cambodia, to the ditches and villages of post-1994 Rwanda. As groups are mobilized on the basis of identity,

> *When the language of future threats is combined with dehumanization, demonization, and zero-sum logic, then children and women become threats to be eliminated – from the gas chambers of Nazi Germany, to the killing fields of Pol Pot's Cambodia, to the ditches and villages of post-1994 Rwanda.*

such traits as ethnicity, religion, language and caste become organizational resources in the political and economic arenas.[6] This mobilizational process is facilitated by the permeative character of ethnic identity, which is described by the foremost scholar of ethnic politics Donald Horowitz as having a tendency to 'seepage'.[7] The ethnicization of social, political and economic life coincides with the politicization of ethnicity, which together serve to crank up the tensions between identity and conflict, and raise the stakes sharply in all confrontations. It adds volatility to every social, political and economic interaction across identity boundaries.

■ 1.5 A CAVEAT: DOUBLE MINORITY COMPLEXES

A straight demographic definition of a majority and minority group is sometimes problematic. Identity groups also need to be put into regional and socio-psychological contexts. This is evident for example in both Sri Lanka and Northern Ireland. The fact that the Sinhala language and culture have no centre outside Sri Lanka has been used by political entrepreneurs to create both a siege mentality and a regional minority complex among the Sinhalese. Although the Sinhalese are a majority within Sri Lanka, many perceive themselves to be a minority in relation to the 50 million Tamils of southern India. Thus, the categorization of groups into minority Tamils and majority Sinhalese masks a phenomenon that could be termed a "double minority complex". This exercises considerable influence on the perceptions and behaviour of both the Sinhalese and Tamil parties to the conflict, in particular by intensifying their sense of threat, raising the stakes of inter-group

---

6 - See for example: Milton Esman, *Ethnic Politics*; D.L. Horowitz, *Ethnic Groups in Conflict*; Paul R. Brass, *Ethnicity and Nationalism: Theory and Comparison*; and Kenneth D. Bush, *Cracking Open the Ethnic Billiard Ball: Bringing in the Intra-Group Dimensions of Ethnic Conflict Studies*, 1996.
7 - Horowitz, ibid.

competition and subsidizing intransigence. A senior diplomat in Sri Lanka's capital, Colombo, summed it up well: "there are three minorities in this country: the Tamils, the Muslims and the Sinhalese". To the extent that this condition affects behaviour within the Sinhalese community, the demographically defined minority and majority categories within Sri Lanka are inverted. Similarly in Northern Ireland, the Protestant community (the majority community in Northern Ireland) perceives itself as a minority from an all-Ireland perspective, while the Catholic community sees itself as a minority in a narrower Northern Ireland perspective. These examples should remind us of the variations in the perceptions and interpretations of such empirical "facts."

■ 1.6 ETHNICITY, EDUCATION AND NATION-BUILDING

Ethnicity continues to be a central point of reference in relations between different groups of people, and most, if not all countries are home to a range of minority groups. There is a great deal of ethnic heterogeneity within contemporary states, despite the implicit claims to homogeneity of culture and identity. Traditionally, education systems have played a key role in maintaining this fictive image of cultural homogeneity. Coulby (1997) highlights some of the ways in which education has been used in the service of cultural homogenization, including the invention and use of a canon of "national literature" and the promulgation of a common national language – two essential components in what has been called the "naturalization" of citizens. Churchill (1996) goes further to suggest that the traditional notion of the state embodied a set of assumptions that simultaneously claim and construct linguistic, cultural and political homogeneity. Schooling may contribute to this process by constructing and imposing a common culture, founded on a common language, a shared sense of history and destiny, and more broadly, a common set of expectations and behaviours rooted in a sense of civic loyalty. Whether the end result is assimilation or integration depends on both the way schooling is structured and the content of the curriculum (both hidden and explicit).

In other words, the "naturalization" of citizens is a process that may be either integrative or disintegrative. In a liberal view of the world, the end result is a society based on tolerance and respect for difference. However, this same process may also generate the opposite outcome: intolerance, jingoism, and a fear and rejection of difference.

Through the liberal lens, the principal task of public schooling, properly organized and delivered, has traditionally been to create "harmony" within a nation of divergent peoples. Public schooling is viewed as an investment in a social contract the benefits of which are believed to accrue not only to the individual who experiences schooling but also, and perhaps more importantly, to the wider society.

But the current challenge of education in many countries, especially newly established ones intent on forging a national identity, is to maintain peace within their own borders, while fostering tolerance of their often very divergent neighbours.

It is possible to identify historical examples of these processes. The development of mass education systems towards the end of the 19th century played a role in unifying nations at a time when the democratic franchise was being extended. This was as true of "old" societies, such as Britain, where the schools could promulgate tradition and history, and "new" societies such as the United States where schools were expected to act as part of the "melting-pot" to fuse a multitude of migrant communities into American citizens. Towards a somewhat different purpose, but following essentially similar processes, the nascent USSR education served as a mechanism for constructing "Soviet man" (Bowen, 1981). In contrast to the melting pot model of the United States, schooling in Canada used the metaphor of a multicultural "mosaic" in which differences were recognized and highlighted, rather than overlooked and blended. The results of these models were mixed, but sufficient to dampen widespread violence – though this generalization should not obscure or minimize the violence inflicted on the aboriginal peoples of Canadians in the residential school system.[8]

A further case is illustrated in the conflicts between Albanians and Serbs in Kosovo. To counteract Albanian attempts to affirm their minority national identity, the Serbian government adopted a policy of assimilation, eliminating teaching programmes in the Albanian language and introducing a unified curriculum and standardized textbooks across the country, measures that many blame for the ensuing strife. In its report to the Committee on the Rights of the Child in 1994, the Yugoslav government admitted that it was encountering major problems in the education of Albanian children in the provinces of Kosovo and Metohijo. Parents refused to send their children to schools working according to the "legitimate programme of the Republic of Serbia". Instead, Albanian children attended non-accredited parallel schools, treated by the Government as illegal. In an alternative report submitted to the Committee, a non-governmental organization points out that a number of important institutions in the educational system were shut down in 1994, including the Institute for Albanology and the Academy of

---

8 - The best and most recent source of information on the residential school system in Canada may be found in the wealth of research commissioned for the Royal Canadian Commission on Aboriginal Peoples. *People to People, Nation to Nation,* Report of the Royal Commission on Aboriginal Peoples (Hull, Quebec: Canada Communications Group-Publishing, 1996). See especially *Volume 1: Looking Back, Looking Forward* which addresses how "Church and government leaders had come to the conclusion that the problem (as they saw it) of Aboriginal independence and 'savagery' could be solved by taking children from their families at an early age and instilling the ways of the dominant society during eight or nine years of residential schooling far from home. Attendance was compulsory. Aboriginal languages, customs and habits of mind were suppressed. The bonds between many hundreds of Aboriginal children and their families and nations were bent and broken, with disastrous results." The rampant physical and sexual abuse of aboriginal children is receiving increasing public attention as past victims are confronting their abusers in highly publicized legal cases.

Two Snapshots

The Central Asian Republics of the former USSR provide two interesting snap shots of nation-building at two points in time under very different sets of circumstances (Akiner, 1997).

Snap Shot One: When these territories came under Soviet control they were carved up into separate Republics. A range of strategies were employed to build national identities, and education was one of the tools. Some of the larger communities were accorded privileges, such as access to key positions in society and politics. Other communities were accorded certain rights, including educational and linguistic rights. Smaller communities were, at various times, subsumed within larger groups or "reclassified" bureaucratically out of existence (with many resurfacing following the exit of the Soviet regime). Other efforts to create common "national" identities included the creation of national languages and the compilation of national histories that were selective and presented within the wider Soviet framework. In particular, while the Republic was described as providing the national identity, the Soviet Union provided the identity of citizenship – which created political tensions that reverberate into the present. Clearly, there was a more explicit-

ly coercive aspect to the process as seen in the suppression of Islam.

Snap Shot Two: With the implosion of the Soviet Union, the Republics gained independence. The newly opened political and social space allowed the creation of very different ideas on nationhood. Not surprisingly, this was a two-fold process based on the rejection of the Soviet-imposed conceptions of identity, and the search for "indigenous" sources of collective identity and community. In this second wave of nation-building, there is, therefore, a resurgence of national cultures (some previously repressed), and a rewriting of national histories. Some republics are experiencing a resurgence of Islamic schools and the teaching and use of Arabic. All are occurring in an environment in which new histories contest the old, challenging the established European/Russian superiority. Consequently, the nation is being rapidly reinvented, or simply invented. This is not to deny the legitimacy of the newly independent States, but to see the processes that all States go through. Furthermore, many of these processes can be addressed through the education system and many are addressed most efficiently in this way.

Sciences and Arts of Kosovo. Educational and professional activities in the Albanian language were no longer allocated government funds, teaching aids in Albanian were not published and the major Albanian publishing house, Rilindja, was closed down. The curriculum and the approach of teachers in the official schools were highly politicized.

There can be no doubt that the schism in education in Kosovo was a major contributor to the upsurge of violence that reached its horrifying zenith in 1999. The point to be emphasized here is that the systematic ethnic cleansing undertaken by the Serbian military forces in late 1999 was in no way a spontaneous event. The precursor to abuse on such a massive scale is the systematic dismantling of the social, political and economic institutions that provide order and stability for a community. This was certainly the case in Nazi Germany, and in Cambodia under Pol Pot.

2. THE TWO FACES OF EDUCATION

■ 2.1 NEGATIVE

Education is often used as a panacea for a broad spectrum of social ills, from racism to misogyny. While the impact of such initiatives has been mixed, their starting premise is the same: that formal education can shape the understandings, attitudes, and ultimately, the behaviour of individuals. If it is true that education can have a socially constructive impact on intergroup relations, then it is equally evident that it can have a socially destructive impact. Because more energy tends to be expended on the examination of the positive face, rather than the negative face of education, it is useful to begin by considering some of the ways in which education has exacerbated intergroup hostility under conditions of ethnic tension.

■ 2.1.1 The uneven distribution of education

Innumerable historical cases can be identified where ethnic groups – and more broadly, social groups – have been denied access to educational resources and, therefore, excluded from full participation in the economic and social life of a country. Such obstacles have both an immediate and longer-term impact on the socio-economic status of the "affected groups." Because education has increasingly become a highly valued commodity, its unequal allocation has been a serious source of friction that has frequently led to confrontation. It also shows how the powers of the state can become "ethnicized," that is, used to advance the interests of one group at the expense of others, as happened when the Serbian authorities reduced the number of places in secondary schools reserved for Albanians in Kosovo.

The discrimination evident in policies and practices that deny access to educational opportunity is, typically, only the tip of the iceberg. It may, for example, coincide with the implementation of quotas to restrict public employment. Or it may coincide with a crackdown on student political organizations.

Restricted access to education should be viewed as an indicator of deteriorating relations between groups. As such, it should be viewed as a warning signal that should prod the international community to initiate what the World Bank would call a "watching brief" so that it might anticipate and respond to further deteriorations before it is too late.

In ethnically stratified societies, privileged ethnic groups usually attain higher average educational levels than members of subordinate ethnic groups. Several factors underlie this pattern. First, educational attainment is enhanced by a privileged background, and students from advantaged ethnic origins benefit from the educational, occupational and economic attainments of their parents. Second, dominant social groups use the educational system to secure their privilege across generations. Because of their cultural and political domination, educational selection is based on criteria that favour their offspring. Third, dominant ethnic groups may control the political processes by which school systems are funded and structured and are able to promote those schools attended by their children or their own educational districts. As a result of these factors, students from advantaged social origins do better in school and obtain more schooling which, in turn, enables them to obtain more desirable occupations (Shavit Yossi, 1990).

During the colonial era, European powers

often employed the standard divide-and-rule tactic of giving certain minority groups access to education so that they could act as local functionaries. At independence, such groups possessed the professional and administrative skills needed to manage the affairs of state – as was the case in many former British colonies such as Sri Lanka, India and Sudan.

In Rwanda, for example, Catholic missionary schools openly favoured the Tutsi minority and actively discriminated against the Hutu from the late 1800s. During the 1920s, the church set up 'special schools' to educate Tutsi as the future leaders of the country and state schools were also established to train Tutsi as support staff for the colonial government. This preferential treatment continued throughout the 1930s and 1940s. One government-funded school in Nyanza, the *Group Scolaire*, even had a minimum height requirement for admission, which, of course, worked to the disadvantage of the Hutu, who tend to be shorter (Newberry, 1988). The Tutsi were almost exclusively admitted to the *École Astrida*, the only existing secondary school, where they were taught to regard themselves as an aristocratic class destined to rule (Chrétien, 1992). While the Hutu received only enough education to enable them to carry out menial jobs, the Tutsi gained a political, administrative, cultural and economic monopoly on power (El Pais, 1997).

Stereotyping in textbooks and by teachers has also been an issue. Textbooks of the German and Belgian colonial periods emphasized the physical differences between the Hutu and the Tutsi, linking physical appearance and intellectual capacity according to prevailing racist doctrines. Such books praised the intellectual capacities of the Tutsi and classified the Hutu as unintelligent, meek and suitable for manual work (El Pais, 1997).

Similarly in Burundi, as a result of decades of discrimination in the educational system, a 'social pyramid' was created with the Tutsi monopolizing the most important positions within and outside the government. Because

First grade math text book in Bulgaria: Count how many words there are in this sentence: "I am grateful to the party for it leads my country to beautiful radiant life and vigilantly protects us from war."
Library of Congress, Country Studies - Bulgaria, June 1992.

of restrictions placed on the admission of Hutu children to secondary schools, "by 1988 only a tiny fraction of the Hutu population had the requisite skills for employment in the modern sectors of the economy" (Stavenhagen, 1996).

■ 2.1.2 Education as a weapon in cultural repression

Taken to an extreme, such repression can be termed 'ethnocide'. This can be defined as "the process whereby a culturally distinct people loses its identity as a result of policies designed to erode its land and resource base, the use of its language, its own social and political institutions, as well as its traditions, art forms, religious practices and cultural values" (Stavenhagen, 1990).

Newly independent governments in Africa often attributed great strategic importance to education as a means of maintaining political command and control. After independence, missionary schools in southern Sudan were taken over by the state and, from 1964, all foreign missionaries were expelled. Schools became totally Arabized. Staff from northern Sudan were recruited for every school supervisory post in the south and every secondary school was removed to the north. The Southern intelligentsia opposed to such Arabization was forced to flee to Uganda and Zaire or to the bush where they established counter movements (Stavenhagen, 1996). In extreme, and not uncommon cases of violent conflict, schools have been used as sites for press-ganging child soldiers and attacking teachers.

In many post-colonial societies, the curriculum remains strongly Euro-centric and completely ignores the local culture. Only infrequently is there an "acknowledgement that the colonized people should be heard from, their ideas known" (Graham-Brown, 1994, quoting Jagdish Gunadara). New generations thus become estranged from their own cultures. According to one analysis, many schoolchildren attending missionary schools in Rwanda in the 1950s were not even aware of the existence of the mwami; a glaring knowledge gap as he was their king (Linden, 1977).

Language is an essential element in the maintenance of ethnic and cultural identity and may be, in some cases, the only test for the existence of an indigenous people. "Through its language, a given group expresses its own culture, its own societal identity; languages are related to thought processes and to the way the members of a certain linguistic group perceive nature, the universe and society" (Stavenhagen, 1996). In many cases, the imposition of a dominant language on ethnic groups (both inside and outside the formal school system) is a repressive act, both in intention and outcome – for example the resistance to Afrikaans schooling during the apartheid era. In such cases, groups have sometimes taken up arms to protect their cultural and linguistic rights. It would, however, be a grave mistake to see every effort to impose a common language on a linguistically diverse population as an aggressive cultural act. In Senegal, as described later in this study, it has had a unifying impact. A critical factor in determining whether it unifies or divides is the manner in which other languages are treated. To the extent that they are acknowledged formally and informally to be an important part of the collective national identity, potential tensions may be diffused.

A similar dynamic is evident in the conflict between the Turkish State and the Kurdish minority in eastern Turkey. Kurds are not allowed to use their language in schools and have been subjected to corporal punishment for doing so. Teachers themselves have been dismissed for permitting Kurdish to be spoken in their classrooms. Kurdish children are discriminated against in schools, and often arbitrarily given poor grades. Kurdish publications have been officially banned and professors at university have been imprisoned for conducting research on Kurdish issues (Graham-Brown, 1994).

The existence of a national language can sometimes ease inter-ethnic relations and help eliminate the preconceptions one group has of another (Nsibambi in UNICEF, 1992). However, carrying out an assimilist policy through

"History is a pack of lies about events that never happened told by people who weren't there".

coercion against the will of an ethnic group will obviously provoke dissent (Stavenhagen, 1996).

■ 2.1.3 Denial of education as a weapon of war

Once relations between ethnic groups have deteriorated to the point of violent conflict, the closure and destruction of schools is used as a weapon of war to erode civilian support processes and to punish insurgents in ways that will compromise irremediably the future of their families and their ethnic groups. This kind of intellectual starvation tactic is a violation of basic human rights.

During the conflict in Mozambique 45 per cent of the primary schools were destroyed, and in Rwanda 66 per cent of the teachers fled or were killed. During and after the Intifada, Israel forced the closure of schools for Palestinian children in Occupied Territories, in some cases for two years or longer. And for those children who participate voluntarily or forcibly in armed conflicts, schooling is virtually non-existent. According to one study in Peru for example, of the 107 children in the Sendero Luminoso's Sello de Oro base camp who took advantage of the Repentance Law, only two could speak Spanish, and none could read or write.[9]

Informal education may also be disrupted by militarized conflict, as the fabric of society is stretched and torn. As a community is forced into a survival mode, and as basic social and cultural institutions are challenged, the normal transmission of skills and knowledge from parents and community to children is often interrupted.

■ 2.1.4 Manipulating history for political purposes

Graham-Brown points out that the control of a government by an ethnic group often leads to "the construction of a version of history ... which heightens the role of that group at the expense of the others ... Suppression of events or cultural ideas ... viewed as subversive or divisive is also common"(Graham-Brown, 1994).

---

9 - From World Vision International, *The Effects of Armed Conflicts on Girls*, p. 16.

But what do we mean when we say that history is 'constructed'? As the critical thinker George Santayana put it, "History is a pack of lies about events that never happened told by people who weren't there." In other words, 'history' is a process by which certain stories and events are highlighted while others are minimized or ignored. One particular set of facts (or 'lies') is agreed upon tacitly and given social sanction and the political seal of approval. It is important to stress that a critical analysis of history does not simply superimpose one set of 'facts and events' for another set. A critical historiography recognizes that there are competing sets of facts and multiple interpretations of events. However, not all histories are equally valid or legitimate. An obvious example is the effort by those who would have us believe that the mass murder of approximately six million Jews by the Nazis either never occurred or is exaggerated. Even a cursory critical assessment of such an argument reveals the political motivations of its contemporary advocates. In some senses, theirs is an 'anti-history' which attempts explicitly to erase empirically verifiable events for base political interests.

It is appropriate here to continue with the Nazi example to highlight one way in which the schooling system and other public institutions were used by the Nazi regime to 'normalize' internal oppression and unthinkable systematic violence. Ordinary Germans and those who worked in state institutions eventually internalized rules of exclusion, thereby alienating such groups as Jews, gypsies and homosexuals. It was then a small step from exclusion to dehumanization to 'extermination'. Education systems legitimized the most appalling events and ideas – from eugenics to an 'Aryan' state. Although many ordinary people came to accept such authoritarian rules, real control came not from acceptance, but from the failure of individuals to reject them. The role of the educational system in legitimizing such actions cannot be overestimated. Authoritarian regimes do not just bypass the critical functions of the education system, they subvert them to their own ends.

...the distortion of history takes place intentionally and unintentionally both through acts of commission as well as omission.

It is important to emphasize that the distortion of history takes place intentionally and unintentionally both through acts of commission as well as omission. If Nazi Germany is a case of an intentional act of manipulation and distortion then the invisibility of pre-colonial Africa from mainstream history is a prime example of distortion through omission. The same can be seen in the historical exclusion by dominant African groups of non-dominant African communities, as well as subjugated groups like the Dalits or tribal peoples in India who are seen as having no great past or history. Indeed, the 'great men' of history have been heroes of war, rather than the heroes of peace. Each of these features of mainstream study of history have a profound effect on our understanding of the present and the future as well as the past.

The study of geography, as well as history, has been drawn into ethnic politics. In 1992, for example, Vidya Bharati prepared a new set of history textbooks that were to be used in schools in Indian states controlled by the BJP, the principal extremist political party. It was noted that in BJP-sponsored textbooks:

> "The revivalists depict the Mughals as foreigners and oppressors, and interpret Indians' achievement of freedom from English rule as but the latest episode in a long ongoing struggle to free India from foreign influences. Muslims are, by this interpretation, the contemporary incarnation of the Mughal pattern of dominance." (Vidya Bharati, 1992)

Military conquest and changes in political control have led to the imposition of new names for old places by the new occupiers. In Israel for example, old Palestinian village names are replaced by Hebrew names. In the Aegean, Turks and Greeks clash over name changes in Cyprus and other contested islands. In the Balkans, the ethnic cleansing of village names followed the ethnic cleansing of villages. Geography texts and classes can serve to legitimize such conquests through the use of politicized nomenclature.

Under conditions of inter-ethnic tension, national elites often force teachers to follow curricula or use textbooks that either homogenize diversity and difference or worse, present it as a threat to be feared and eliminated. The history of inter-group relations is often cast as an unbroken and unvarying process of conflict. In the hands of capable ethnic manipulators, past events (factual and fictional) are used to illustrate historical wrongs, humiliation and exploitation. The single objective of such individuals is the mobilization of tribal support for their respective political projects. Past histories and current instances of intergroup cooperation and intermarriage are frequently expunged from public memory, as the hostilities of the present (again factual and fictional) are projected onto the past. Heterogeneity is presented as a threat to the coherence and unity of the political entity. Yet, the real danger is that the centralization and homogenization of educational policies, historical pasts and institutions can lead to greater levels of disintegrative tendencies. Obviously the situation varies from case to case. But educators and political actors have an obligation to recognize and address such issues in a more concerted and systematic manner than has been the case in the past.

In the Balkans, the ethnic cleansing of village names followed the ethnic cleansing of villages.

■ 2.1.5 Manipulating textbooks

Ethnic intolerance makes its appearance in the classroom in many ways. One issue gaining increasing attention in many parts of the world is the militaristic nature of much of the history taught in schools and the relative neglect of the gains civilizations have made in peacetime. Wars frequently occupy a prominent place in history curricula and are sometimes the central theme of the literature studied as well. This emphasis can lead to violence being accepted as a legitimate expression of political power. This strong focus on historical bloodshed does little to foster a climate of tolerance.

Textbooks have often been shown to contain negative ethnic stereotypes, as in the case of Rwanda.[10] Similarly, in Hitler's Germany, textbooks incorporated a racist doctrine, legitimizing the exclusion of groups such as Jews and the Roma.

UNESCO has recently concluded that the tendency of history textbooks to exalt nationalism and address territorial disputes correlates with the xenophobia and violence found in many countries today. What is taught in history class and how it is taught is highly political and can foster either animosity or peace.[11] A review of the textbooks used in the segregated schools of Sri Lanka in the 1970s and 1980s, for example, found Sinhalese textbooks scattered with images of Tamils as the historical enemies of the Sinhalese, while celebrating ethnic heroes who had vanquished Tamils in ethnic wars.[12] Ignoring historical fact, these textbooks tended to portray Sinhalese Buddhists as the only true Sri Lankans, with Tamils, Muslims and Christians seen as non-indigenous and extraneous to Sri Lankan history. This version of national history, according to one commentator, has been deeply divisive in the context of the wider state.[13]

Arabs are accorded a small place in Israeli textbooks in comparison to other historical forces. Napoleon and the French Revolution occupy more pages than Arabs in history textbooks. Quantity does have a quality value, as it dictates the number of class hours dedicated to the teaching of the topic. Israeli history textbooks, like the teaching materials of most other nations, strive to enhance patriotism among new generations. One way they do this is to emphasize Jewish-Zionist narrative, which centres on the Jewish heroes who fought and overcame the local Palestinians and survived despite the hardships of the land and the strength of foreign regimes.

This emphasis, as Professor Ruth Firer of the Truman Institute at the Hebrew University of Jerusalem points out, does little to decrease the enmity between the people involved (Firer, 1998). Some new history textbooks in the Hebrew language offer a revisionist way of looking at the formal history. These texts, written by a group of historians who are called 'Post-

---

10 - El Pais, 1997.
11 - UNESCO, 1998.
12 - E. Nissan, 1996.
13 - Ibid.

Zionists' and 'the New Historians', include facts that have been excluded from the national consensus, trying to look at the past and present from outside, rather than from inside the Israeli Jewish community. Their revised version of Zionist narrative is largely disputed by the Israeli public, however, and their material is usually found in the appendices of textbooks, rather than in the main chapters.

◼ 2.1.6 Self-worth and hating others

One South African parent, in a survey conducted in Soweto, South Africa, stated that apartheid education made blacks see themselves as inferior: "You have to see yourself as the poorest of the poor because, according to the South African government, that is the way God has made you. Our education does not make you question this pre-supposed status" (Graham-Brown, 1991). Similarly, an analysis of the method and contents of Soviet education, provided by Peeter Mehisto, Counsellor to the Ministry of Education of Estonia (UNICEF 1993) is also particularly revealing. Citing the "intellectual and moral poverty" of Soviet education, he states that:

"Despite its rhetoric, Soviet-style education denied personal responsibility, subjugated the individual and served bureaucratic and military interests. It favoured top-down, fact-based force-feeding which focused on the need for the correct answers as opposed to the need to teach skills for learning. Education was centred on the teacher, not the learner. This stifled individual initiative. It gave no rewards for individuality, but instead rewarded conformity and passivity" (Graham-Brown, 1991).

This description of formal education processes is probably accurate in relation to many other settings – North, South, East and West. How deeply this kind of instruction affects the individual's ability to make considered judgments and to take responsibility for his or her own actions is an important question. However, as a starting point, it is essential that we acknowledge the linkages between a child's sense of self-worth and his or her susceptibility to manipulation. An inability to make reasoned judgements leaves children vulnerable to exploitation, whether as child soldiers, or the next generation of ethnic mobilizers. In a masterful study on the origins of genocide and other forms of mass group violence, Irvin Staub addresses, among other issues, the linkages between low self-esteem and scapegoating.

"Blaming others, scapegoating, diminishes our own responsibility. By pointing to a cause of the problems, it offers understanding, which, although false, has great psychological usefulness. It promises a solution to problems by action against the scapegoat. Devaluation of a sub-group helps to raise self-esteem. Adopting an ideology provides a new world view and a vision of a better society that gives hope. Joining a group enables people to give up a burdensome self, adopt a new social identity, and gain a connection to other people. This requires action, but it is frequently not constructive action."[14]

Intolerance is also expressed in less tangible ways. Teachers from the majority culture may display negative attitudes towards minority students, expect very little from them and fail to recognize and encourage their individual talents. Testing, moreover, is often geared to majority cultures, or is left to the discretion of individual teachers or schools. The lack of control over the process can result in gross injustices. Girl pupils from minority groups must also contend with additional gender-based discrimination – if they have had the good fortune to get to school in the first place.

◼ 2.1.7 Segregated education to ensure inequality, lowered esteem and stereotyping

In South Africa, the education system sustained and perpetuated the apartheid system.

---

14 - E. Staub, *The Roots of Evil: The Origins of Genocide and Other Group Violence.*

According to the logic of the system, education had to be segregated because the level of instruction deemed "appropriate" for blacks was far lower than that required by white people. According to Graham-Brown, "because of its pivotal role in sustaining the apartheid system, education has always been a central political issue, and is perceived by all parties to the conflict as a terrain over which political struggle occurs" (Graham-Brown 1991). Unequal, segregated education was both a reflection of, and a contribution to, the repressive apartheid system. The symbiotic relationship between apartheid schooling and apartheid politics, meant that all ameliorative efforts were doomed to failure, unless they addressed both simultaneously.

Scholars have found that colonial education policies in Rwanda introduced a more marked stratification between ethnic groups than had existed in the past. As stratification was intensified, ethnic distinctions were sharpened. These processes, moreover, helped to foster the emergence of a new and broader identity group (Hutu) based on the resentment of the dispossessed. (Newbury, 1988).

In countries in the North where there has been ethnic strife, minority ethnic groups have often been limited to an inferior education in separate (implicitly or explicitly) educational systems – as in the early days of conflict in Northern Ireland, and the inner city areas of France and the United States. As education is increasingly seen as an important resource for success in today's technological world, its unequal provision is increasingly likely to be a cause for tension and conflict.

In Northern Ireland,[15] segregation along religious lines was almost total until the 1980s. Some early commentators even blamed the Troubles on religiously segregated schooling and argued for the development of integrated schools. Segregation, they said, emphasized differences and encouraged mutual ignorance and, perhaps more important, mutual suspicion. Catholic school-leavers in Northern Ireland have been shown to have, on average, lower qualifications than their Protestant counterparts and hence reduced job opportu-

nities. A government-sponsored study in 1973 found that this stemmed, in good part, from unequal funding arrangements. State schools, overwhelmingly attended by Protestants, received full state funding, whereas independent Catholic schools had to rely largely on their own resources. The exclusionary character of the political system and the corresponding state mechanisms were based on the maintenance of the Protestant ascendency that had taken firm root over the four decades since the partition of Ireland. The "social contract" between the state and the majority Protestant community represented a collaboration to maintain a particular social, political and economic order of exclusion. The prominent Irish historian Patrick Buckland described State-society relations as follows:

"Since parties and majorities require tangible rewards and individual satisfaction as well as words and organization, the whole government machinery became geared to ensuring the contentment and continued support of the different sections of the party. Discrimination became built in to the processes of government and administration, as the government pandered to Protestant and Unionist whims large and small – whether they concerned the upkeep of a particular piece of road, the educational interests of the Protestant Churches or the local defence of Unionism."[16]

While the situation varies from case to case, the results of the discrimination and humiliation suffered by the individual children of ethnic minority groups include under-achievement and alienation. Minority children often leave school feeling inferior, or at least convinced that the majority groups in their society consider them inferior. Equally dangerous, children of the majority groups learn to think of themselves as being better than others. They are not taught to respect the values and traditions of the

---

15 - Discussion on Northern Ireland is drawn from Gallagher, 1998.
16 - Patrick Buckland, *A History of Northern Ireland.*

minorities with whom they live. Minority children who drop out of school are left without the tools needed to realize their full potential in a world where literacy is becoming more and more essential for survival. Many children leave school with a profound distrust of the institutions of the State in which they live and, because of the poor quality of education they have received, they are particularly susceptible to the machinations of ethnic mobilizers. Their lack of preparation also makes them vulnerable to being institutionalized or coming into conflict with the law. On a societal level, the discrimination endured in schools can plant the seeds for ethnic divisions and conflict.

Just as Frantz Fanon recognized the need to decolonialize the minds of formerly colonized peoples, so it is essential that we recognize the need to de-segregate the minds of formerly segregated peoples.

2.2 POSITIVE

2.2.1 Conflict-dampening impact of educational opportunity

In the United States, confronted by ethnic tension in the late 1960s, the Government tried to establish greater equality of provision, and set up bussing programmes, affirmative action programmes (including Head Start for pre-school children) and later, the so-called magnet schools in inner-city areas; schools given extra funding and equipment in the hope that their superior education would attract white students back to these areas. Since the early 1990s, the United States has expanded school choice by allowing the creation of charter schools; schools established by communities, parents and educators to accommodate their diverse requirements. These schools receive public funds and are accountable for their results to public authorities, offering low-income families a degree of educational choice formerly unavailable to them and eliciting a high degree of parental participation. While many inequities remain in educational provision in the United States, and while not all educational policies adopted have been entirely successful, the clear demonstration of political will to make changes has, no doubt, contributed to preventing ethnic tensions escalating out of control in the United

States.[17] Similarly, on the west coast of the United States and elsewhere (e.g., Canada) bilingual education programmes also appear to have had a positive impact in increasing inter-group understanding, and decreasing community tensions.

2.2.2 Nurturing and sustaining an ethnically tolerant climate

Catholics and Protestants in Northern Ireland were educated in segregated schools until 1981. The Government has recognized the damage caused by ethnically segregated school systems and has progressively equalized the funding of Catholic and Protestant schools. Considerable resources have been devoted to a number of 'bridge-building' initiatives aiming to give children of each religion the opportunity to learn about each other. Education for Mutual Understanding (EMU) for example, is a compulsory part of the school curriculum. According to Tony Gallagher of Queens University, Belfast, it is clear that conciliatory educational policies in Northern Ireland have contributed to mitigating the conflict, although schools could be used even more efficiently to further community relations.[18] Maintaining a focus on Northern Ireland, the next section continues the discussion of the creation of an ethnically tolerant climate with specific reference to the 'desegregation of the mind'.

2.2.3 The de-segregation of the mind

Just as Frantz Fanon recognized the need to decolonialize the minds of formerly colonized peoples, so it is essential that we recognize the need to de-segregate the minds of formerly segregated peoples.[19]

Communities cannot desegregate until the idea of de-segregation has taken root – not necessarily in every member of a community, but in enough individuals to develop a sustainable critical mass of interest in fundamental

---

17 - A. Gallagher, 1998.
18 - Ibid.
19 - F. Fanon, *The Wretched of the Earth.*

change. As illustrated in the examples of Northern Ireland and the United States, schools have played a pivotal role in this process over the years. This is possible because of the intimacy of the relationship between teaching and learning. This creates the space within which the character, or biography, of a student may be affected (for good or for ill) in ways that are reflected in their relationship to and their behaviour in the world outside the walls of the classroom. When schooling exercises a positive impact on the processes of de-segregation, it does so through that intimate connection between biography and geography.

> *When schooling exercises a positive impact on the processes of de-segregation, it does so through that intimate connection between biography and geography.*

The case of Northern Ireland provides a useful point of reference for assessing the role and impact of de-segregated education on the dynamics of peace and conflict in ethnicized settings. In this case, we have seen education play a critical role in enabling members of the middle class to transcend sectarian divisions. Since the Second World War, the Catholic middle classes have expanded and diversified as a result of improved educational opportunities and the demands of new industries for professionally trained administrators and middle managers. An outward-looking, more liberal attitude in the economic realm coincided with a parallel process in the religious realm with the liberalization of the Catholic church – exemplified during the period of Pope John XXIII (1958-63) and the changes promulgated by the Second Vatican Council, including encouragement of ecumenism. A perceived liberalizing trend in the Catholic church, coupled with political and economic liberalization, allowed the rise of less sectarian, more technocratic leaders in Northern Ireland such as Terence O'Neill, and in the Republic of Ireland, including Sean Lemass. Not surprisingly, the ensuing fear of change was harnessed to the anti-liberal, anti-ecumenical programme of protest that allowed the rise of Ian Paisley.

Even within those areas of high sectarian conflict such as Belfast, middle class moderates are challenging the sectarianism of segregated neighbourhoods by moving into integrated areas like Malone Road in South Belfast and parts of North Belfast. There appears to be a steady migration from the staunch Catholic and republican neighborhoods in West Belfast where many had sought protection during the worst violence of the early 1970s.[20] Since then, there has been a move toward integration in owner-occupied neighborhoods, particularly by the Catholic middle class who are less afraid to move into Protestant areas – that is, into middle and upper middle class Protestant areas

The gradual moves away from segregated education, the inclusion of Education for Mutual Understanding in the curriculum and other liberal trends within the school system reinforced – and were reinforced by – liberalizing trends in the political and economic sphere in Northern Ireland, Ireland, and Europe more broadly. When a conjuncture of such forces exists, a mutually reinforcing positive dynamic sets in. Where such forces do not exist, the challenge to is to nurture them individually to create a synergy in which the collective impact is greater than the sum of the individual parts.

■ 2.2.4 Linguistic tolerance

A sensitive handling of linguistic issues can also contribute to the building and maintenance of peaceful relations within and between different ethnic groups. In Senegal, for example, where there are 15 different linguistic groups and where Islamic and Christian populations have long co-existed peacefully, no civil wars have occurred since independence from France in the 1960s (Stavenhagen, 1996). One important factor in explaining the relative 'ethnic peace' of that case is that after independence French was made the official

---

20 - John Morrow of Corrymeela estimates that previously the composition of South Belfast had been approximately 80 per cent Protestant and 20 per cent Catholic, whereas now it has been estimated to be evenly divided between the two groups. Such dramatic changes were also evident in North Belfast (Kenneth Bush, personal interviews, Belfast).

language in a conscious effort to prevent linguistic conflict, while Diola, Malinke, Pular, Serer, Soninke and Wolof were declared to be national languages. Not only are these languages a critical part of the curriculum, they are also used in radio and television broadcasts and literacy campaigns. While Wolof could have been declared the country's official language, given its predominance, this was never attempted as it would have offended different ethnic groups.

Many other governments have now recognized the importance of making school a less alien place for ethnic minority children. One solution is to use their mother tongue in the classroom, at least in the early grades. As well as improving their chances of learning, mother-tongue instruction helps children to be proud of the language they have used from birth and reinforces their self-esteem, sense of identity and sense of belonging. It also prevents language loss, which may have been a continual process since the dawn of civilization, but is a kind of linguistic Darwinism, representing a loss of a unique perception of the world, a way of life and a knowledge system. As such, it diminishes our common humanity.

Mother tongue provides the child with the best medium to learn at early stages; hence literacy in their first language precedes literacy in the second. Moreover, acquisition and development of the first language assists in the successful acquisition of the second (dominant, national or majority language), which means that first language enhances and does not detract from the learning of a second language.

While teaching a national language in schools is part of nation-building, there is no evidence that teaching of minority languages necessarily diminishes a sense of political unity. In fact, compelling smaller groups to accept the linguistic dominance of the majority is a major cause of ethnic tensions and political instability, as has been seen in Kosovo.

The use of first language in schools helps to develop an inclusive ethos. It is difficult to marginalize children with different languages, cultures and histories if these are integral parts of the education process. Bilingual education

will help ethnic groups participate as citizens of the countries in which they live, presenting them with the knowledge and means to defend their interests as well as revitalizing and strengthening their own cultures. If thematic areas from the dominant culture are then brought into the education process in a non-conflictual and non-substitutive way, this can assist the process of understanding. More importantly, in the context of majority/minority; dominant/subordinate relations, it is the majority and the dominant that really require understanding of the minority/subordinate cultures (Aikman, 1997).

The Committee on the Rights of the Child has taken up the issue of languages on different occasions in its review of States' initial or periodic reports. It stressed, for example, the need to allocate resources to translate school materials into minority languages in Myanmar (*Myanmar IRCO, Add.69, para. 39*). It encouraged the UK Government to provide further support to the teaching of the Irish language in schools in Northern Ireland (UK IRCO, Add.34, para. 33). It has frequently encouraged States Parties to take steps to ensure that teachers capable of working with minority children are trained and their services made available in every region of a given country. It has also acknowledged the need for minority groups to learn the majority language to ensure access to secondary and higher education on an equal footing (China IRCO, Add.56, paras. 19 and 40).

There are costs involved, including developing learning materials and training teachers in bilingual education approaches, and some countries feel that bilingual education is simply not 'cost-effective'. But these costs should be weighed against the price society pays for high dropout and repetition rates in schools where such language programmes do not exist. In conflict-prone areas, insensitivity to the cultural and linguistic needs of ethnic minority groups has been shown to have a very high price indeed.

■ 2.2.5 Cultivating inclusive citizenship

There is an important positive role for intellectual leaders to play in developing new concepts of the state, and its relationship to the citizen. And there is a need to move away from the idea that a particular ethnic group, perhaps claiming descent from a common ancestor, is the only legitimate holder of state power and toward ideas of nations as multi-cultural entities, though with a distinctive cultural profile. The objective of this exercise is to create a shared understanding of, and connection to, the state through an expanding process of inclusion rather than exclusion. By highlighting commonality and shared experiences and objectives, the intention is to create the common ground necessary for constructive and supportive bonds to develop within and between civil society and the state.

The Council of Europe, aware that, in the interests of regional stability, history teaching across the former Soviet Union must be reformed, is supporting work on a new history textbook for children of the Caucasus. Known as the Tbilisi Initiative, the project brings together historians in Armenia, Azerbaijan, Georgia and Russia. Their task is to compile a textbook that is not "written in a triumphalist, polemical or even vindictive style," but rather "neutral and realistic, and free of ideological and political stereotypes." Military issues will be dealt with, but not given undue prominence. The textbook is meant to replace the standard textbook for the region, A *History of the USSR*, which had completely ignored the history of the Caucasian peoples.

There have been recent efforts on the part of the professional education community to establish a set of international standards for civics education. These standards go to the heart of the necessity for compromise. Instead of attempting to establish the rights and privileges of minority populations, they attempt to delineate the obligations and responsibilities for all populations, majority as well as minority.

The proposed international professional guidelines include standards of many kinds. They include standards for curriculum content, for example, presenting different views of history and different opinions on its contemporary relevance. They include a set of terms to identify different levels of critical thinking – being able to identify a concept; describe it; explain it; evaluate a position about it; take and/or defend a position concerning it. They include a set of standards for participation in civics, being able to manage a conflict, build a consensus, influence others by moderating someone else's view, etc. Lastly there are standards proposed for terminologies used in civics – civil society, constitutional rights, private opinion, citizenship obligations and so on. These components constitute an international precedent, establishing for the first time an international standard for curriculum excellence in civics.

The purpose of establishing an international professional standard is to actively establish a set of principles against which each country and each local curriculum authority may measure its own civics curriculum (Center for Civics Education, 1994; CIVITAS, 1995; Center for Civics Education, 1997; Heyneman, 1995a, 1995b). If this effort proves successful, then national authorities around the East and Central Asia region will have a professional benchmark against which to judge local curriculum authorities. The opposite also pertains, and local and minority curriculum authorities will have an international benchmark by which they can measure the degree to which national curricular authorities are fair and balanced in their views of history and civil rights and responsibilities. Of course, whether those in authority will agree to impose such externally-created benchmarks is another matter entirely.

■ 2.2.6 The disarming of history

One possible negative impact of education is the manipulation of history for political ends. The opposite side of this same coin can be seen when education serves to disarm history. In this context, all children have a right to know and to understand their own personal story, that is, they have a right to know their own place in a larger history. Not only do young people need access to these stories, but more importantly, they must be able to read them critically so that they can become active participants in writing their own stories. This requires the cultivation of skills that will enable them to analyze and assess those facts and events that are presented to them as the foundation of their historical selves. Too often, history is presented as a rigid concept and children are led to believe that their place in history and their associated roles cannot be challenged, let alone changed. For example, if children are taught that they are members of a besieged community, the idea – let alone the opportunity – to develop neutral and interdependent relationships with outside communities is very unlikely to arise.

Critical historiographic skills are essential if young people are to be able to identify the intersection between their personal stories and larger collective histories. Only when young people realize that histories are constructed rather than given, can they even begin to contemplate challenging and changing the behaviour that poisons inter-group relations.[21] Further, the Machel Report recommends that national teachers' unions in areas where ethnic conflicts have occurred hold consultations on how curricula can contain manifestations of nationalism, anger and aggression. The curricula should try to help children and young people see the effects of war on themselves, their families and their communities:

> "The contents and process of education should promote peace, social justice, respect for human rights and the acceptance of responsibility. Children need to learn the skills of negotiation, problem solving, critical thinking and communications that will enable them to resolve conflicts without resorting to violence."[22]

In addition, education systems should be encouraged to include instruction about the fallacies and perils of ethnic prejudice and the duty of individuals to be alert to their own tendencies to engage in ethnic stereotyping.[23]

Deeply rooted ideas and vested political interests often make it difficult to address the manipulation of historical representations – especially in textbooks. This issue is particularly difficult when governments or dominant groups stress singular national identities. Yet, as discussed in Section One, individuals always have more than one identity by which they define themselves. This multiplicity of identities does not necessarily detract from national loyalty. In this context, we need to ask: what is the role of education in legitimizing notions of multiple identities as normal, not as a sign of disloyalty to the state? Educationalists should explore ways of giving voice to these heterogeneous identities.

■ 2.2.7 Education for Peace Programmes

Graça Machel has suggested 'Education for Peace Programmes' as one kind of educational initiative that might have constructive peacebuilding impacts.[24] Education for peace programmes are being promoted by UNICEF and are reaching many thousands of children in war-scarred countries, in Burundi, the Republic of Congo, El Salvador, Guatemala, Honduras, Lebanon, Liberia, Mozambique, Nicaragua, Sri Lanka, Sudan and former Yugoslavia. However, while such programmes are *reaching* thousands of school children, the nature or depth of their impact is less clear. Similarly, public media are sometimes involved in these processes, especially to reach out-of-school children and other sectors of the community. It is hoped that an educational approach will contribute to the development of local peacebuilding capacities, since, as already noted, any solution will be unsustainable unless it is developed and supported by state and non-state actors within the war-torn societies themselves. Such positive measures could be implemented throughout an ethnic conflict-affected society, including the schools, the media, judicial system, the security sector, the unions and so on.

Although peace education and human rights courses are essential for cultivating broader understandings of rights and possible options, experience from some countries suggests that introducing them in a context of systematic discrimination is but one ingredient in

---

21 - UN, 1996a, *op. cit.*
22 - Ibid, para. 255.
23 - Project on Ethnic Relations, Princeton 1994.
24 - UN, 1996a, *op. cit.* (para 255-258).

the recipe for change. More broadly, school systems themselves must become more equitable and democratic, starting from the experience children have in the classroom. Lessons characterized by rote learning and the absence of open debate, where rules must be obeyed without question, undercut children's confidence and inhibit their participation as active members of their societies. Similarly, children cannot be expected to learn the real meaning of democratic principles when their families and communities have no way of making their views and feelings known to the school and staff and no assurances that, if they do, these will be taken seriously. The process of education, teaching and learning, as well as the way schools function as institutions, carry their own powerful messages. Democratic, participative and inclusive schools are an important part of children's experiences.[25] Unfortunately, however, this is an ideal that is rarely present in the North, let alone the South. The fundamental question is how can a critical education system be nurtured within non-democratic, pseudo-democratic or transitionally democratic political systems?

■ 2.2.8 Educational practice as an explicit response to state oppression

There are many lessons that can be drawn from the case of apartheid South Africa – lessons concerning what to do, as well as what not to do. In this case, we see an instance where Roman Catholic schools admitted black pupils, and thereby defied the government's prohibition on integrated education. One is struck by a number of contrasts. First, Church schools in different settings have been forces for progressive change as well as for the maintenance of an unjust status quo. Second, we have seen that governments often engage in the self-interested manipulation and politicization of the institution of schooling.

But the South African case suggests an example of how resistance to this process can symbolize and galvanize forces for constructive change. This was possible because of the space that existed between state and non-state supported schooling systems. As the state con-

centrated its resources on the schooling of its white population, non-state actors stepped into the breach to provide education to non-serviced areas (i.e. black, and to lesser degree, coloured areas). A similar situation developed in Sri Lanka as the formal mechanisms of state became increasingly ethnicized in favour of the Sinhalese majority. The neglect of the Northern and Eastern Tamil regions created the space for church schools to enter the educational fray. In these cases, we see that governmental neglect can create opportunities within which alternatives to violence can be developed and articulated.

To the extent that the schooling system is able to do so, it assumes a very important role in the peacebuilding process – not necessarily in the oppositional function it plays, but in its ability to maintain and articulate credible alternative visions of the future; visions that are inclusive, tolerant, liberal, democratic and just. This is precisely why authoritarian states tend to target the school system as soon as they acquire sufficient means.

Under these conditions, Northern actors are sometimes in a difficult position when they are required to choose between the constructive engagement approach of working through a repressive regime in an effort to initiate reforms, and the civil society approach of working for change from the bottom up.

---

25 - J. Gundara, 1998.

3. TOWARDS A PEACEBUILDING EDUCATION

"Some thrash in agony on the ground, while others lie motionless. The captured and wounded are punched, kicked and dragged through the dust. Some are blindfolded and guns are held to their heads. I am watching this while standing against a crumbling concrete wall near a school in Jabalia Camp (a Palestinian refugee camp in the Gaza Strip). The people before me are Palestinian children – the youngest perhaps four, the oldest no more than 17. They are playing a game they call Arabs and Jews". (Semeniuk, 'War Babies', 1995)

As some of the negative impacts of education have already been discussed and illustrated above, this section places more emphasis on the type of education that would self-consciously and systematically seek to have a positive peacebuilding impact within regions characterized by ethnic tensions. More specifically, it introduces and sketches out the parameters of what it calls *peacebuilding education*. This is seen to be the next step in the evolution of peace education, which has tended to use a rather narrow recipebook approach that is heavily dependent on workshop training in mediation and negotiation skills, conflict management, non-competi-

> *Peacebuilding education – like peacebuilding itself – would be a bottom-up rather than top down process driven by war-torn communities themselves, founded on their experiences and capacities. It would be firmly rooted in immediate realities, not in abstract ideas or theories. It would be applied, immediate, and relevant, which means that it cannot be restricted to the classroom.*

tive dialogue and so on. There is no doubt that such skills can have an important dampening impact on specific episodes of confrontation and threatened violence. For this reason, peace education programmes should be encouraged. However, while they may help people to deal with the immediate and proximate triggers of violence, they do not necessarily address the deeper, structural causes. The development of a peacebuilding education is based on the need to expand the scope of our educational approaches in ways that allow us to respond to both the manifestation of violence and its causes.

To move in this direction requires us to understand education in its broadest sense: formal, informal and non-formal; content and teaching methods; arts and sciences; child-centred and adult-centred. The point of engaging the education process in the task of peacebuilding is not to homogenize the curriculum or to create uniform students from different social or cultural groups. Rather, it seeks to initiate or support an educational process that allows students to articulate, accommodate and accept differences between and within groups, particularly (though not exclusively) in regions characterized by latent or manifest violence. This entails a distinct two-fold process that nurtures and constructs positive inter-group relations while marginalizing and deconstructing negative inter-group relations. As Neil Postman has put it, this requires the existence of shared narratives *and* the exclusion of narratives that lead to alienation and division. (Postman 1996).

While this insight appears to apply across cases and cultures, Postman focuses largely on the education systems of Western liberal democratic societies that possess educational, social, economic and political institutions that are more robust than those found in most regions characterized by identity conflict. Despite considerable obstacles to changing the education systems in liberal democratic societies, there are at least the institutional networks to translate societal desires into action – elected school boards, parent-teacher associations, municipal elections, and so on. However, in ethnic conflicts where violence has been protracted such institutional networks are usually weakened, creating many more challenges to the initiation and development of educational systems with sustainable peacebuilding impacts. Most important is the need to cultivate positive and mutually reinforcing linkages between the formal educational system and the sub-cultures or islands of peace within society.

■ 3.2 THE CONTEXT

The specific impact of conflict on formal and informal education depends on the nature and dynamics of violence. While ethnic conflict may ethnicize education (affecting curriculum content and narrowing the diversity of the student population) the general disruption caused by widespread militarized conflict may also have a positive impact by opening opportunities to challenge restrictive ideas, practices, and roles.

From Somalia and Sri Lanka to Peru and Palestine, for example, women and girls are breaking from restrictive societal expectations to assume leadership roles in peace movements, NGOs and politics. The opening of the social space in conflict-prone areas within which girls and women may challenge and overcome obstacles to their advancement is reflected in this recollection by a 16-year-old girl in Sudan: "Now my father tells me: 'Rebecca my girl, you must try to read very hard because in your future no one will try to help you, but you will help yourself, and us also." [26]

Stable social institutions may not be child or woman-friendly. In these cases, challenging such stability may be both necessary and desirable, as it creates the space for women and children to break out of confining traditions. Typically, the ability to encourage and affect such far-reaching societal and institutional change is reduced once a conflict comes to an end, and the space that allowed women to flex their muscles is usually reclaimed. As we think about the potential peacebuilding role of education in war-torn and war-threatened societies, therefore, we should look for opportunities as well as constraints. And reconstruction should be seen as an opportunity to transform conventional education systems.

It is essential to recognize that there is rarely a complete divide between ethnic communities. Even in the most extreme cases, the violence is neither undifferentiated nor impenetrable. Based on years of studying conflict and discord in the Middle East, Edward Azar concludes:

> "Conflictual and cooperative events flow together even in the most severe of intense conflicts. Cooperative events are sometimes far more numerous than conflictual ones even in the midst of intense social conflict situations. However, conflictual events are clearly more absorbing and have more impact on determining the consequent actions of groups and nations (and one might add, on determining the outsider's impression of the conflict). Cooperative events are not sufficient to abate protracted social conflicts. Tension reduction measures may make the conflict more bearable in the short term, but conflict resolution

---

26 - World Vision, *The Effects of Armed Conflict on Girls*, A discussion paper prepared by World Vision for the UN Study on the Impact of Armed Conflict on Children (Geneva, Switzerland: World Vision International, July 1996).

involves a far more complex process than mere conflict management."

(Azar, 1985).[27]

The point to be emphasized within the context of constructive educational initiatives is that even within severe conflicts there are spaces for peacebuilding; spaces that are often dangerous, tenuous and fluid, but very much in existence.[28] The failure to search for the spaces within which cross-group linkages are formed is a missed opportunity.

The variability of cross-community interaction in ethnicized settings has been recognized by some Northern Irish scholars who have pointed to what they call situational variation in relationships, and functional integration. Darby writes:

When it comes to educational initiatives that are intended to have beneficial impact on inter-group relations, a useful starting point is the recognition that one size never fits all. In some cases, one size fits no one.

"Complete avoidance between Catholics and Protestants is impossible in most parts of Northern Ireland. Most people may 'mingle with a conscience of the differences between them,' but they do mingle. In most places it is possible for members of the two groups to develop relationships without abandoning their separate basic allegiances. They may drink in the same pubs, use the same shops, work together, and belong to the clubs... Even during periods of tension, it is possible for a Protestant and a Catholic, each of whom would regard the other with suspicion if seen in his district at night, to suspend animosities and continue to work at the same work bench during the day."

(Darby 1991)

The degree of contact and mixing in Northern Ireland often depends on the demographic mix of a neighbourhood or the immediate setting. The advantage of such situational variations is that they allow changes to evolve at their own speed.

One of the most important features to highlight from the case of Northern Ireland is the variety of instruments within the educational strategy adopted to address heightened tensions and the polarization of communities. The response was not to attempt to desegregate the system in one fell swoop. In that case – and in most cases – this was neither possible politically, nor would it have been effective socially. Recognizing that different communities would have different levels of receptivity to change, we see a set of graduated or calibrated educational initiatives beginning with the initial efforts, introduced on a voluntary basis, to build themes related to positive community relations into the curriculum. The second initiative, contact programmes, moves from a school-specific focus of curriculum development to one that begins to work on the linkages between school and society. And finally, the third initiative sought to develop integrated schools to serve both Protestant and Catholic students.

When it comes to educational initiatives that are intended to have beneficial impact on inter-group relations, a useful starting point is the recognition that one size never fits all. In some, one size fits no one. Consequently, the effectiveness of an educational initiative increases to the extent that it is flexible and responsive. It is important to note that the inter-group contact that is facilitated through

---

27 - For this reason, NGOs may do more than simply encourage cooperation (or fund cooperative projects) in the hope that some kind of 'demonstration effect' or 'trickle-down effect' will ultimately lead to peace. They can also engage directly in the task of encouraging the transformation of those structures and processes which condition social, political and economic interaction – so that the obstacles to peace and cooperation are removed.

28 - These are precisely the spaces that catalyze the activities of a variety of community groups in conflict situations around the world: citizens' committees like the Batticaloa Peace Committee in Sri Lanka; 'mothers' groups campaigning for the end of disappearances like the Mothers of Acari in Brazil; inter-communal groups like PACE, Corrymeela, the Cornerstone Community, and the Peace People in Northern Ireland; and many others. These are crucial points of intervention and islands of peace. They exist, but to fully exploit them requires sensitivity, creativity and diplomacy.

such programmes is a necessary but not a sufficient requirement for peacebuilding. The chances of success for such efforts increase to the extent that they are supported by parallel structures that foster understanding and, more importantly, empathy between groups. This would be reflected in both the content and process of schooling, but also in the mutually supportive linkages forged between those inside and those outside school walls.

The inability to resist ultimately subsidizes such oppressive mechanisms. State-sponsored and anti-state-sponsored terror batters a population first into submission, then into acquiescence.

■3.3 CULTURES OF FEAR AND COPING MECHANISMS

In a masterly study of state terror and resistance in Latin America, Juan Corradi and his colleagues have demonstrated how systematic human rights abuse may create a culture of fear that embeds political apathy and inaction into the social fabric of society.[29] This work points to mechanisms that inhibit civil society in resisting violence. The inability to resist ultimately subsidizes such oppressive mechanisms. State-sponsored and anti-state-sponsored terror batters a population first into submission, then into acquiescence. Social order and control is achieved by instilling and manipulating fear at profound human, political, and social cost and the mechanics of this process are well-recognized and pervasive. The violence inscribed on the bodies of victims becomes a message communicated to society as a whole.[30] Civil societies have developed a variety of mechanisms to cope with the various forms and levels of violence generated by bad governance and human rights abuse. Such mechanisms are important for understanding why and how one population may suffer in relative silence, while another may organize, resist and rebel. The examination of cultures of fear in Latin America in the 1980s reveals the cultural and anthropological components of coping. The fear to act because of the constant threat of punishment is transformed into a subconscious, cultural predisposition not to act. It becomes better to ignore,

forget, or selectively see the world, than to live with the corrosive omnipresence of fear.

In such settings, the school system can be a force for change by sustaining hope, courage, and imagination in the minds of students. However, for the large part, under the conditions described above, the regime's efforts to control the population involve the subordination of all public institutions – especially schools – to its political objectives. Both the content and the process of schooling become a means through which the regime attempts to shape ideas and affect behaviour in ways that glorify its own project and inculcate obedience. Violence or the threat of violence within the school becomes an essential ingredient in this process. While dissent may remain in hidden forms within schools, the overarching form of response is silence.

■3.4 DISTINGUISHING PEACEBUILDING EDUCATION FROM PEACE EDUCATION

In any discussion of peacebuilding education, there is a clear need to go beyond approaches based predominantly on academic study and training. First, academic study is too often too removed from the real world, application, and the practical consideration of implications or impact. Second, the idea of training smacks of an approach premised on externally generated and imposed solutions, that fails to recognize the possibility that culturally and place-specific peacebuilding capacities may well exist, and be more appropriate and sustainable. It is significant to note that within the international community the language of training (external intervention with quick exit strategies) pre-

---

29 - Juan E. Corradi, Patricia Weiss Fagen and Manuel Antonio Garreton, editors, *Fear at the Edge: State Terror and Resistance in Latin America*. See also Carolyn Nordstrom and JoAnn Martin, editors, *The Paths to Domination, Resistance and Terror*.
30 - E. Scarry, *The Body in Pain: The Making and Unmaking of the World*.

dominates over the language of education (implying longer-term commitment).[31]

As a starting point, it is useful to note a number of substantive differences between peace education and peacebuilding education. Peacebuilding education would be driven by those affected by militarized violence, not by the largely Northern, white, academic elite that drove efforts to get peace issues onto the academic agenda in the 1960s, '70s, and '80s. Peacebuilding education – like peacebuilding itself – would be a bottom-up rather than top down process driven by war-torn communities themselves, founded on their experiences and capacities.

Like peace education, peacebuilding education might include facts and figures related to contemporary militarized violence. And it would include the teaching of conflict management techniques and critical reading skills and the cultivation of the values of cultural tolerance and non-violence. However, peacebuilding education would be firmly rooted in immediate realities, not in abstract ideas or theories. It would be applied, immediate and relevant. This means that it cannot be restricted to the classroom. It might include community projects involving children and adolescents from across ethnic borderlines or inter-ethnic economic development projects. For example, in Mozambique this might include assistance in rebuilding schools where damage to the educational infrastructure left two thirds of the primary school age children without access to education.[32] The joint UNICEF/Government of Sri Lanka programme, Education for Conflict Resolution, provides another example of how the process and content of new curriculum packages might draw on and resonate with the cultural environment within which they are set – even when the environment is bifurcated into Hindu and Buddhist.[33]

3.5 GUIDING PRINCIPLES AND THE ROLE OF EXTERNAL ACTORS

If education is to have a sustainable peacebuilding impact, then it will have to be driven by those individuals and groups within war-torn, war-born, and war-threatened societies themselves. This means that external actors must assume supporting and facilitating roles – roles with which they may not be comfortable or familiar. This does not suggest that external actors should reduce their development assistance, rather that they should devolve decision-making authority and, where necessary, support the development of the managerial capacity needed for war-affected populations to regain administrative control of both public and private educational initiatives. The identification, cultivation and support of national and local peacebuilding capacities require a sustained commitment, as well as a willingness to take risks, experiment, and learn from mistakes. The same features that characterize peacebuilding education must also characterize the role of external donors, namely that it:

1. is a process rather than a product
2. is long-term rather than short-term
3. relies on local, rather than external, inputs and resources
4. seeks to create opportunities rather than impose solutions

If these are accepted as the guiding premises of peacebuilding education, then Southern voices must drive the process at the front end, not after the formulation of frameworks and approaches; and not only for the implementation of someone else's solutions.

3.6 THE GOALS OF PEACEBUILDING EDUCATION

Peacebuilding is an activity that is ultimately defined by its impact (Bush 1995, 1998). This is why such a broad range of development activi-

---

31 - For a clear example, see Eileen F. Babbitt, 'Contributions of Training to International Conflict Resolution', in Zartman and Rasmussen, *Peacemaking in International Conflict*, US Institute of Peace, Washington, 1997.
32 - UNICEF, *State of the World's Children 1996*.
33 - Details of the Education for Confect Resolution Programme are provided in UNICEF's *State of the World's Children 1996*. What is not clear from the description is where the Muslim and Christian minorities fit into the curriculum, if it incorporates common Buddhist and Hindu principles. Nor is it clear how it addresses the intra-group animosities, particularly caste-based, and regional tensions.

ties can fall within the peacebuilding rubric. Just as not all development initiatives are peacebuilding initiatives (indeed, some may aggravate tensions), neither do all educational initiatives have a positive impact. As discussed above, some educational initiatives have had an unqualified negative impact. The following hypothetical example from Bush (1998) highlights the need to clearly distinguish the developmental impact from the peacebuilding impact of education projects because it may be that development failures may still have beneficial peacebuilding impacts.

An education project may fail to produce students able to pass state-wide exams, but may succeed in reducing tensions between particular social groups by creating and institutionalizing a non-threatening and constructive environment that increases neutral contact and decreases misunderstanding by dispelling stereotypes and misconceptions.[34] Unless there is sensitivity to the peacebuilding and social reconstruction achievements of this hypothetical project, then it would be cast as a failure. The converse also holds true. It is possible that a project may succeed according to pre deter mined developmental criteria but fail in terms of a beneficial impact on peace. To continue with this hypothetical example, an education project may indeed succeed in increasing the number of students passing the state-wide examinations. However, if the bulk of those students are members of one particular social group, then the project may exacerbate inter-group tensions by underscoring the perception that one group is being privileged at the expense of another.

Under the current rules of the development game, the development success/peacebuilding failure would get funding again, whereas the development failure/peacebuilding success would not be funded again. This is a problem. Until we develop and apply the appropriate means to recognize such impact, our ability to understand (let alone reinforce) the positive linkages between development initiatives and peacebuilding will be hampered.[35]

Given the relative neglect of education issues within the evolving peacebuilding and reconstruction project, the intention in the next section is to introduce what are seen to be the central points of reference for this crucial area of action. These should be expanded and refined through engagement and input from those on the front lines of education and conflict.

...demilitarization of the mind...

One of the cental objectives of peacebuilding education is the demilitarization of the mind. The meaning of demilitarization is inextricably connected to our understanding of militarization. As Thomas Hobbes pointed out centuries ago:

> "Warre consistith not in battel onely, or the act of fighting, but in the tract of time wherein the Will to contend by Battel is sufficiently known as the nature of foule weather, layeth not in a shower or two of rain; but in an inclination thereto of many days together; so the nature of war, consisteth not in actuall fighting, but in the known disposition thereto, there all times there is no assurance to the contrary."[36]

Hobbes recognized that an understanding of militarization should not be restricted to the actual fighting, but the predisposition to fight. In the contemporary context then, the militarization of society refers not only to the increasing prevalence and influence of military/paramilitary actors, and the influx of weapons into the streets and fields of a region. It also refers to the tendency – or inclination in Hobbesian terms – for inter-group relations and conflict to be defined narrowly in military terms. This typically coincides with an increase in military-related expenditures, and a military crackdown on dissent within civil society and on both armed and unarmed political opponents. More

---

34 - In Northern Ireland, this is an objective of Education for Mutual Understanding (EMU) programs. The larger task is the incorporation of EMU objectives into all educational programmes.
35 - One effort to do this through the development of Peace and Conflict Impact Assessment (PCIA) may be found in Bush, *A Measure of Peace: Peace and Conflict Impact Assessment of Development Projects in Conflict Zones.*
36 - Thomas Hobbes, *Leviathan.*

generally, militarization is a phenomenon in which political problems come to be represented as military problems, thus justifying military solutions.

The demilitarization impact of education may be direct – for example, through the dismantling of the cultural and socio-psychological predisposition of an individual to use violence as a first, rather than last, resort. It may, however, be indirect, in the sense of altering collective views and responses of society that may be reflected in the decreased prominence of military weapons in social, political, and economic life; the gradual delegitimization of a gun culture; and the evolution of non-violent modalities of conflict management

…problematization…

Education is commonly understood to provide the means for the acquisition of appropriate knowledge, and thence for development. While this may be true, it is also a rather mechanistic, building-block way to view the nexus of education, knowledge, and development. Education also has a critical role to play by encouraging individuals to question taken-for-granted understandings and facts. It can help an individual recognize the need for change. This is an essential step before one can begin to contemplate – let alone formulate – alternatives. It might be understood as a process of opening a world closed by the oppressive immediacy of militarized conflict. Education may serve to cultivate more positive, critical orientations that explore the connections between taken-for-granted facts or understandings and the reinforcement of those structures and processes that maintain and perpetuate under-development and violent conflict. This critical thrust of education opens possibilities for thinking and acting in ways that both challenge orthodoxies and struggle for transformation and empowerment in the fullest sense. One of the roles of peacebuilding education is also to challenge convention and thereby to initiate alternative (sometimes opposing) thought processes in a domino dynamic. This objective will not necessarily produce tangible alternatives. As Postman explains:

"…despite some of the more debilitating teachings of culture itself [ed. note: in this particular, context a culture of violence], something can be done in school that will alter the lenses through which one sees the world; which is to say that non-trivial schooling can provide a point of view from which what is can be seen clearly, what was is a living present, and what will be as filled with possibility". [37]

…articulation of alternatives…

The passage that opens this section – describing Palestinian boys beating each other as they play Arabs and Jews – is a chilling example of how societal and political pathologies can he reflected, perpetuated and learned through play. The same types of pathologies may be conveyed in different forms within a classroom. The loss of childhood in militarized violence means that the gradual process of socialization, the development of confidence, and sense of responsibilities are short-circuited. The hard world of violence violates the once-protective shell of childhood, as the child is thrust into the horrors of war. They are shot at and shelled; they are kidnapped and forced to slave and fight for militarized groups; they are raped and girls are forced to act as wives in rebel groups; children are forced by military groups to inflict atrocities on their family members and neighbours so that they will be ostracized and have no where to go but that group.

Peacebuilding education (during and after violent conflicts), no less than peacetime education, must be a place that articulates and demonstrates alternatives. Children take their cues from the legacies of hate and distrust that permeate a post-conflict setting. It would be naive to believe that the existence of a place of tolerance, dignity, and respect will meet and defeat a militarized culture in a direct confrontation. The fundamental objective is to show children that alternatives exist, *if choices are made*. While these choices might be hard and painful, they do exist. This, then, is a message of empowerment: you have a choice; you

---

37 - Neil Postman, *The End of Education*, p. x.

have the power to change your world in a way that affects your place and role – past, present and future.

…changing the rules of the game…

As noted above, a central question for the current study is the degree to which education can play a constructive role – not in altering the content of group identities but in altering the rules of ethnic interaction. That is, peacebuilding education has a positive impact to the extent that it can alter the basic rules that guide the interaction of identity groups in all spheres of life – social, commercial, political, and so on. It is not automatic that increased cooperative contact in one sphere or realm will necessarily spill over into other realms. Thus, peacebuilding education seeks to build bridges between groups and communities that have been separated and polarized by violent conflict. The guiding logic of interaction would shift from intolerance, suspicion and hopelessness to tolerance, trust, and hope. So too would it seek to re-humanize those who have been de-humanized.

…delegitimization of violent force as a means of addressing problems…

Part of the challenge of demilitarizing the mind is the delegitimization of the use of violence as a means of addressing problems. As violence filters into more and more dimensions of an individual's life, behaviour and expectations adapt to accommodate it. In the face of the breakdown of other institutions that once provided security and meaning, recourse to violence for self-protection and advancement becomes increasingly tempting.

The demilitarization of war-torn societies cannot be separated from the need to demilitarize the peacebuilding initiatives of the international community.[38] To the extent that international initiatives accept the violence-based political and military realities on the ground in conflict zones, and to the extent that this induces the international community to work through the boys with guns, international assistance may serve to subsidize the militarization of the environment. At a macro-level

this includes treating warlords or military commanders as if they were legitimate representatives of terrorized populations (e.g., in Somalia and Bosnia). At a micro-level, this includes the use of militarized factions for the protection or delivery of supplies. In the case of Somalia, the power of the gun has displaced – but not erased – more traditional, and legitimate, forms of authority based on discussion and compromise. The challenge for peacebuilding education is to *de*legitimize gun-based authority structures, and *re*legitimize traditional or alternative authority structures, while maintaining an ability to work on the ground. Peace-nurturing initiatives should be planned and implemented in a manner that reinforces constructive local initiatives.[39]

■ 3.7 THE IMPORTANCE OF RE-MEMBERING

The term 're-membering' is used by Carolyn Nordstrom to describe a particular process by which a community reconstructs itself culturally, physically *and ontologically*. She explains:

"The disruptions of war far exceed the physical casualties and material destruction. If the foundations of culture are jarred in a war turned dirty, ontology is thrown open to question and people's sense of reality itself is rendered tenuous.

---

38 - For an excellent discussion of how to avoid or minimize the militarizing impact of humanitarian interventions see Gayle E. Smith, "Relief Operations and Military Strategy," in Thomas G. Weiss and Larry Minear, eds., *Humanitarianism Across Borders: Sustaining Civilians in Times of War* (Boulder and London: Lynne Rienner Publishers, 1993). For a more recent critical assessment of some of the dilemmas confronting the international community see Dylan Hendrickson, "Humanitarian Action in Protracted Crises: The New Relief Agenda and its Limits," *Relief and Rehabilitation Network* (RRN) Network Paper #25, Overseas Development Institute, April 1998.
39 - Two fascinating examples of the successful nurturing of an indigenous peace process may be found in Somaliland. See Rakiya Omaar, Somaliland: One Thorn at a Time,= *Current History,* May, 1994, and the Mennonite Central Committee of Canada (MCCC), Submission to the Canadian Council for International Cooperation Foreign Policy Review: A Framework for our Common Future.

If we accept the premise that reality is socially constructed, then the disruption of the basis of social relations and the shared epistemological truths on which it rests necessarily imperils people's ability to continue to construct a significant reality... identity itself is then jeopardized." [40]

It is in this context that peacebuilding education should seek to re-member, or reassemble the ontological fabric of a society – a symbolic socio-political re-establishment of boundaries, and an affirmation of bodies and identities. Remembering can provide socio-conceptual coherency – the identification of something rendered whole. The reverse side of the process of re-membering should also be recognized: returning the limbs to the body politic rests on the recognition of stories of immense cruelty against the bodies of average people, a process capable of inculcating the very terror it seeks to overturn. [40]

...modalities of change...

Some of the mechanics for reorganizing and restructuring schooling systems to meet the special needs of children of ethnic minorities, immigrants and indigenous people, may also increase the likelihood that the goals identified here will result from the education process. As discussed at an Innocenti Global Seminar in 1997, this might include curriculum adaptation; bilingual teaching; after-school or weekend classes; improvements in teacher training; and recruitment and training of teachers from all identity groups. [42]

The specifics of redeveloping education systems depend on the particularities of the case. While the Innocenti Global Seminar suggested that educational structures be decentralized, this may not be efficacious in cases of protracted, militarized, identity-based conflicts where there is a need to develop a sense of national community from a society fragmented by violence. This is especially so in cases where battle lines were drawn between geographically dispersed groups. Somehow a balance must be struck between the maintenance of group difference and group solidarity. The suggestion that parents be involved directly in the schooling of their children is of special importance in peacebuilding education because it provides a channel both for drawing in community resources (which helps to ensure sustainability and relevance) and for engaging the broader education in the peacebuilding process. This participatory element is essential. As Uphoff observed, more important than knowing *how much* participation is occurring is knowing *who is* or is not involved in different kinds of participation. Which groups are less involved in different kinds of decision making, or in different kinds of implementation, or in different kinds of benefits, or in different kinds of evaluation? Women? Youth? Ethnic minorities? Persons living in remote villages? Insecure tenants? ... Is it being done: at the initiative of officials, an NGO or the villagers themselves? With a monetary incentive, or voluntarily, or through coercion? In an organized manner or on an individual basis? Directly or indirectly? On a regular or ad hoc basis? Is the process continuous, intermittent, or sporadic? With a degree of empowerment – how much? [43]

---

40 - C. Nordstrom, *Back Yard Front.*
41 - *Ibid.*
42 - See Maggie Black, Children and Families of Ethnic Minorities, Immigrants and Indigenous Peoples.
43 - Norman T. Uphoff, Monitoring and Evaluating Popular Participation in World Bank-Assisted Projects.

4. CONCLUSION

This discussion does not lend itself to summary in a tidy, compact package. This study will have succeeded if it encourages a more critical thinking about the place of formal and informal education in environments racked by ethnic conflict. As indicated at the outset, the study is only the first cut at an examination of a set of issues that have tended to be relegated to the margins of the analysis of ethnic conflict. To the extent that the negative face of education is acknowledged, the tendency has been to call broadly and generally for more and "better" educational practices. It is clear in this study, however, that the effectiveness of this "more and better" approach will be limited unless it is complemented by an approach that simultaneously dismantles destructive educational practices. To put it bluntly, the "add good education and stir" approach alone will not produce the fundamental changes that are necessary in ethnic conflict-affected societies. This underscores the need to go beyond solutions that are merely additive (add women and stir, add children and stir, add environment and stir) towards solutions that are *transformative* – solutions that change the underpinning logic and structures of behaviour.

The principal difficulty that we face in this context is this: it is easier to add new educational initiatives than to change old ones. Why? Because the change of educational practice is a fundamentally *political* threat in the sense that it challenges structures of authority, dominance and control – in the North no less than the South.

One of the clearest implications of this

To put it bluntly, the "add good education and stir" approach alone will not produce the fundamental changes which are necessary in ethnic conflict-affected societies.

observation is that the transformation of the conditions of ethnic violence will be extremely slow and painful unless efforts include political resources as well as pedagogical and educational resources. The interdisciplinary approach of this study is just a first step in establishing a set of common understandings, mobilizing the necessary range of resources, and breaking away from compartmentalized approaches towards those that are complementary, systematic and sustained. This makes sense both conceptually and practically: complex and multidimensional problems must be matched with multifaceted responses.

The task before us is to fashion a concrete plan of action. The contribution of this study is that it examines the dynamics of the positive and negative impacts of education and identifies some broad guidelines and principles for moving ahead constructively. It is this variability of impact that prompts a number of observations that may help to orient our thinking about education and violent conflict.

- Most obviously: in many conflicts around the world, education is part of the problem not the solution, because it serves to divide and antagonize groups both intentionally and unintentionally.
- Initiatives that focus exclusively on either the informal or formal dimensions of education are doomed to failure because of the potential influence or veto one dimension has over the other.
- While content of curriculum matters (e.g., the misrepresentation of history does have negative impacts whether in Quebec or in

Sri Lanka) so does process. Curriculum packages that espouse tolerance and egalitarianism, but that are delivered within educational structures that are fundamentally intolerant and inegalitarian cancel out much of the potential positive impact.

- This discussion of identity, education and conflict applies to both North and South. Many of the educational institutions in the North are segregrationalist (especially along the lines of class and colour). The most significant difference between North and South is that in the former case, political, social and economic institutions exist to accommodate or defuse dissent and inequity.

It is useful to conclude with an outline of the study.

■ 4.1 THE NEGATIVE FACE OF EDUCATION

The study has examined the following peace-destroying conflict-maintaining impacts of education within specific examples of identity-based conflicts (and non-conflicts!):

- the uneven distribution of education as a means of creating or preserving positions of economic, social and political privilege
- education as a weapon in cultural repression
- denial of education as a weapon of war
- education as a means of manipulating history for political purposes
- education serving to diminish self-worth and encourage hate
- segregated education as a means of ensuring inequality, inferiority, and stereotypes
- the role of textbooks in impoverishing the imagination of children and thereby inhibiting them from dealing with conflict constructively.

■ 4.2 THE POSITIVE FACE OF EDUCATION

In contrast, some peacebuilding and conflict-limiting impacts of education were identified as follows:

- conflict-dampening impact of educational opportunity

- nurturing and sustaining an ethnically tolerant climate
- education and the desegregation of the mind
- linguistic tolerance
- cultivation of inclusive conceptions of citizenship
- the disarming of history
- education for peace programmes
- educational practice as an explicit response to state oppression.

■ 4.3 GUIDING PRINCIPLES FOR PEACEBUILDING EDUCATION

Peacebuilding education:

- is a process rather than a product
- is long-term rather than short-term
- relies on local, rather than external, inputs and resources
- seeks to create opportunities rather than impose solutions.

■ 4.4 THE GOALS OF PEACEBUILDING EDUCATION

- demilitarization of the mind
- problematization
- articulation of alternatives
- changing the rules of the game
- delegitimation of violent force as a means of addressing problems
- re-membering and re-weaving the social and anthropological fabric
- nurturing non-violent, sustainable modalities of change.

The requirements for turning away from inter-ethnic violence are deceptively complex. Basically, this process boils down to the following questions:

- Do shared values exist – in the margins, if not in the mainstream – that would enable communities to live together in peace?
- If they do, are they a sufficient basis for mobilizing inter-group support for the rejection of violence as the principal means of resolving disputes?
- Can they foster behaviour that is participato-

ry and complementary instead of aggressive and competitive?

If the answers to such questions are affirmative, then conditions are ripe for inter-ethnic reconciliation through the nurturing of bonds of solidarity and cooperation. If the answers to such questions are negative, then the challenge is to create the conditions that would allow for such shared values to develop. It is possible that the existence and proper functioning of supranational bodies of arbitration might be a necessary precondition for this to become a reality.

The Mandate of the United Nations is imbued with the hope of achieving these values and lays down ways and means to achieve their universal application. It might well appear that the ideal of peace is a bit high-flown, if not downright unrealistic. Yet, even in the face of the ethnicized and militarized slaughter that characterized much of the early post-Cold War period, peace has become more than an aspiration or utopian endpoint.

Paradoxically, we have seen the struggle to create and sustain a culture of peace in places where we would least expect it: within those 'neighbourhoods' of violence scattered throughout the world. This is particularly evident in efforts undertaken by groups and leaders within civil society, such as the Mothers of the Disappeared in Plaza del Maya and the Nobel Peace Prize laureate 'Peace People' in Northern Ireland. These are cultures – perhaps more accurately, subcultures or nascent cultures – according to which humankind can organize itself. However, this is only possible if there are commonly shared values.

By looking at both faces of education, we develop a clearer understanding of the positive and negative impacts of education in areas prone to ethnic violence. There are very different operational and policy implications of this two-faceted optic. On the one hand, it suggests that by identifying which initiatives do harm we might be better able to 'stop doing the wrong thing'. In contrast, by developing a better understanding of positive impacts of educational initiatives, we can continue to nurture and 'do the right thing'.

Annex - The International Legal Framework

The United Nations Convention on the Rights of the Child (CRC) – ratified by every country in the world but two (Somalia and the United States) – provides the overall framework for any discussion of ethnicity, education and conflict. The CRC and other instruments (see box below) obligate ratifying States to:

- actively prevent discrimination, including on grounds of ethnicity, against children and their families, with additional specific protections for children of minorities and indigenous peoples;
- ensure a right to education without discrimination;
- ensure that education is directed to encouraging respect for human rights, peace, tolerance, non-discrimination and non-violence;
- ensure protection of the child's right to freedom of religion;
- ensure the child's right to diverse information and encourage the positive involvement of the mass media;

- protect children from all forms of physical and mental violence (with specific provisions protecting the child from various forms of violence and exploitation, and protection of the child affected by armed conflict).

Confronted with countries scarred by civil conflicts and racial tensions, and with the rise in xenophobic and racist attitudes in several countries, the Committee on the Rights of the Child, the treaty body responsible for monitoring the CRC, has on several occasions urged States Parties to modify educational systems to conform to the provisions of the CRC. In reviewing the Initial Report of the Federal Republic of Yugoslavia, for example, it stated that, "School curricula materials should be developed, if they do not already exist, which aim at educating children in the spirit of tolerance of and respect for different civilizations." (IRCO, Add.49, para 30). It recommended that the Government of Nigeria "incorporate education on the rights of the child in the school

International instruments relating to ethnic conflicts and education

The main international instruments relevant to this study are:

- Universal Declaration of Human Rights (1948)
- Geneva Convention Relative to the Protection of Civilian Persons in Time of War (1949) – Article 24
- UN Declaration of the Rights of the Child (1959)
- Convention against Discrimination in Education (1962) – Articles 1, 2 and 5
- International Convention on the Elimination of All Forms of Racial Discrimination (1969) – Articles 4, 5(d)(v) and 7
- International Covenant on Economic, Social and Cultural Rights – Article 13
- International Covenant on Civil and Political Rights (1976) – Articles 18.4, 20, 26 and 27
- Declaration on Fundamental Principles concerning the Contribution of the Mass Media to Strengthening Peace and International Under-

standing, to the Promotion of Human Rights and to Countering Racialism, Apartheid and Incitement to War (1978) – Article IV
- Convention on the Elimination of All Forms of Discrimination against Women (1981) – Article 10
- Declaration on the Elimination of All Forms of Intolerance and of Discrimination based on Religion or Belief (1981) – Article 5
- Convention on the Rights of the Child (1989) – Articles 2, 17, 19, 28, 29 and 30
- Declaration on the Rights of Persons belonging to National or Ethnic, Religious and Linguistic Minorities (1992) – Articles 2.1, 4.3 and 4.4
- UN Universal Declaration of the Rights of Indigenous Peoples (1993)
- UNESCO Recommendation Concerning Education for International Understanding, Cooperation and Peace and Education relating to Human Rights and Fundamental Freedoms

curricula, paying special attention to promoting tolerance among all peoples and groups." (Nigeria IRCO, Add.6.1, para. 38. See also Croatia IRCO, Add.5.2, para. 19 and Guatemala IRCO, Add.5.8, para. 30).

The United Nations Special Rapporteur to former Yugoslavia explicitly recognized the connection between violent ethnic conflict and education in a 1996 report (United Nations, 1996b):

> "[The] young generation must develop different approaches to human values than those the world has witnessed ... during the last five years. There is, therefore, great urgency in including human rights education (i.e. an appreciation for tolerance and a multicultural

society) in the curricula of all schools, not only on a voluntary basis but as an important obligation of the different countries' educational systems."

As part of the UN Decade for Human Rights Education, 1995-2004, established under General Assembly Resolutions 48/127, 49/184 and 50/177, governments and non-governmental educational agencies are being urged to establish programmes of human rights education.

In 1995, the United Nations Educational, Scientific and Cultural Organization (UNESCO) endorsed a Declaration and Integrated Framework of Action on Education for Peace, Human Rights and Democracy (see box below). The Framework sets out policies, objectives and action strategies to combat discrimination, vio-

---

Declaration and Integrated Framework of Action on Education for Peace, Human Rights and Democracy, 44th session of the International Conference on Education (Geneva 1994), endorsed by the General Conference of UNESCO at its 28th session (Paris 1995) – Article 2

We, the Ministers of Education meeting at the 44th session of the International Conference on Education... strive resolutely:

1. To base education on principles and methods that contribute to the development of the personality of pupils, students and adults who are respectful of their fellow human beings and determined to promote peace, human rights and democracy;

2. To take suitable steps to establish in educational institutions an atmosphere contributing to the success of education for international understanding, so that they become ideal places for the exercise of tolerance, respect for human rights, the practice of democracy and learning about the diversity and wealth of cultural identities;

3. To take action to eliminate all direct and indirect discrimination against girls and women in education systems and to take specific measures to ensure that they achieve their full potential;

4. To pay special attention to improving curricula,

the content of textbooks, and other educational materials including new technologies, with a view to educating caring and responsible citizens, open to other cultures, able to appreciate the value of freedom, respectful of human dignity and differences and able to prevent conflicts or resolve them by non-violent means;

5. To adopt measures to enhance the role and status of educators in formal and non-formal education and to give priority to pre-service and in-service training as well as the retraining of educational personnel, including planners and managers, oriented notably towards professional ethics, civic and moral education, cultural diversity, national codes and internationally recognised standards of human rights and fundamental freedoms;

6. To encourage the development of innovative strategies adapted to the new challenges of educating responsible citizens committed to peace, human rights, democracy and sustainable development, and to apply appropriate measures of evaluation and assessment of these strategies;

7. To prepare, as quickly as possible, and taking into account the constitutional structures of each State, programmes of action for the implementation of this Declaration.

lence and xenophobia, and to develop students' self-esteem, stressing the last as "essential to social integration...The reduction of failure must be a priority."

The Committee on the Rights of the Child has urged many States Parties to make children's rights principles widely known, including by translating the Convention into all the languages spoken by minorities. They have also suggested that school curricula materials be developed, if they do not already exist, that aim at educating children in the spirit of tolerance of and regard for different civilizations. (United Nations, 1996c). Some of the new States in Central and Eastern Europe have taken steps in this direction.

So sensitive have the inter-ethnic problems become in Europe and Central Asia that NATO is increasingly concerned that inter-ethnic tensions expressed through education could well constitute a risk to peace in the region. The Organization for Security and Cooperation in Europe (OSCE) has established a High Commissioner on National Minorities, based in the Hague (Foundation on Inter-Ethnic Relations, 1997). The High Commissioner has issued recommendations pertaining to the education of the Greek minority population in Albania, the Albanian population in the Former Yugoslav Republic of Macedonia, the Slovak population in Hungary, the Hungarian Population in Slovakia and the Hungarian population in Romania. In 1996, the High Commissioner requested assistance from the Foundation on Inter-Ethnic Relations to work on a possible set of guidelines governing the education rights of national minorities. These guidelines, known as the Hague Recommendations, were published in 1997 and can be added to the many other international conventions and regulations that attempt to identify and to protect the educational rights of children and various sub-populations.

References

ADORNO, T.W., E. FRENKEL-BRUNSWIK, D. J. LEVINSON, and R. N. SANFORD, *The Authoritarian Personality*, Harper, New York, 1950.

ADWAN, S., 'Ethnicity and Conflict: The Role of Education Project - The Palestinian National Authority (PNA)'. Unpublished research paper, UNICEF International Child Development Centre, Florence, 1998.

AHLSTORM, C., *Casualties of Conflict: Report for the World Campaign for the Victims of War*, Department of Peace and Conflict Research, Uppsala, 1991.

AIKMAN, S., 'Intercultural Education in Latin America', in Coulby, D., J. Gundara, and C. Jones, *World Yearbook of Education: Intercultural Education*. Kogan Page, London, 1997.

AKINER, S., 'Melting Pot, Salad Bowl - Cauldron? Manipulation and Mobilization of Ethnic and Religious Identities in Central Asia', *Ethnic and Racial Studies*, 20(2), 1997.

ALLPORT, G. W., *The Nature of Prejudice*. Addison-Wesley, Reading MA, 1954.

ALMOND, G. A. and S. VERBA, *The Civic Culture*. Princeton University Press, Princeton, 1963.

AZAR, E., 'Protracted International Conflicts: Ten Propositions', *International Interactions*, 12:1, 1985.

BABBITT, E. F., 'Contributions of Training to International Conflict Resolution', in Zartman, I. W. and J. L. Rasmussen, *Peacemaking in International Conflict: Methods and Techniques*, United States Institute of Peace, Washington, 1997.

BACAL, A., 'Ethnicity in the Social Sciences'. CRER Reprint Paper in *Ethnic Relations* 3, Centre for Research in Ethnic Relations, University of Warwick, UK, 1991.

BECKER, E., 'Personality Development in the Modern World: Beyond Freud and Marx', in Burns, H. W. (ed.), *Education and the Development of Nations*. School of Education, Syracuse University, Syracuse NY, 1963.

BLACK, M. 'Children and Families of Ethnic Minorities, Immigrants and Indigenous Peoples', *Innocenti Global Seminar Summary Report*. UNICEF International Child Development Centre, Florence, Italy, 1997.

BOWEN, J., *A History of Western Education: Volume 3, The Modern West*. Methuen, London, 1981.

BUCKLAND, PATRICK, *A History of Northern Ireland*. Gill and Macmillan, Dublin, 1981.

BRASS, P., *Ethnicity and Nationalism: Theory and Comparison*. Sage, New Delhi, 1991.

BUSH, K. D., 'Towards a Balanced Approach to Rebuilding War-Torn Societies', *Canadian Foreign Policy*, Vol. III, No. 3, 1996.

BUSH, K. D., 'Cracking Open the Ethnic Billiard Ball: Bringing in the Intra-Group Dimensions of Ethnic Conflict Studies', *Occasional Paper* (9:OP: 1), Joan B. Kroc Institute for International Peace Studies, University of Notre Dame, Notre Dame, 1996.

BUSH, K. D., *A Measure of Peace: Peace and Conflict Impact Assessment of Development Projects in Conflict Zones*. Ottawa, International Development Research Centre, 1998.

CAMPBELL, A., P. E. CONVERSE, W. E. MILLER, and D. E. STOKES, *The American Voter*. University of Chicago Press, Chicago, 1976.

CANTWELL, N., 'Starting from Zero: The Promotion and Protection of Children's Rights in Post-Genocide Rwanda, July 1994 - December 1996', *Innocenti Insights*. UNICEF International Child Development Centre, Florence, 1997.

CARMENT, D. and P. JAMES, *Escalation of Ethnic Conflict: A Survey and Assessment*. Carleton University and Iowa State University, 1996.

CENTER FOR CIVICS EDUCATION, *National Standards for Civics and Government*. Center for Civics Education, Calabasas CA, 1994.

CHALK, F. and K. JORIASSOHN, *The History and Sociology of Genocide: Analyses and Case Studies*. Yale University Press, New Haven, 1990.

CHRÉTIEN, J.P., 'Le défi de l'intégrisme ethnique dans l'historiographie africaniste: le cas de Ruanda et Burundi', *Politique Africaine*. Centre d'étude d'Afrique noire, Université Montesquieu, Bordeaux IV, 1992.

CHURCHILL, S., 'The Decline of the Nation State and the Education of National Minorities'. *International Review of Education*, 42 (4), 1996.

CIVITAS@Prague. *Strengthening Citizenship and Civic Education, East and West*. USIA, Washington DC, 1995.

COMER, J.P., 'Educating Poor Minority Children', *Scientific American*, 29, no. 5, 1988.

CONNOR, W., 'Nation-Building or Nation-Destroying?', *World Politics*, 1972, 24.

CORRADI, J. E., P. WEISS FAGEN, and M. A. GARRETON (eds.), *Fear at the Edge: State Terror and Resistance in Latin America*. University of California Press, Berkeley and London, 1992.

COSTARELLI, S., 'Children of Minorities: Gypsies', *Innocenti Insight*. UNICEF International Child Development Centre, Florence, 1993.

COULBY, D., 'Educational Responses to Diversity within the State'. In Coulby, D. et al. (eds) *Intercultural Education: World Yearbook of Education 1997*. London, Kogan Page, 1997.

COULBY, D., J. GUNDERA, and C. JONES (eds), *Intercultural Education: World Yearbook of Education, 1997*. London. Kogan Page, 1997.

CRAFT, M. (ed.), *Teacher Education in Plural Societies: an International Review*. Falmer, London, 1996.

CREMIN, L. A., *Public Education*. Basic Books, New York,1976.

DARBY, J., 'What's Wrong With Conflict?', *Centre for the Study of Conflict Occasional Paper* 3. University of Ulster, Northern Ireland, 1991.

DARBY, J., *Scorpions in a bottle: conflicting cultures in Northern Ireland*. Minority Rights Group, London, 1997.

DAVIES, P. (ed.), *Human Rights*. Routledge, London, 1988.

DE GUCHTENERE, P., L. LE DUE and R. G. NIEMI,'A Compendium of Academic Survey Studies of Elections Around the World', Update 1, *Electoral Studies*, 10 (3). Elsevier Science Ltd., New York, 1991.

DUNCAN, GREG J., 'Earnings Functions and Non-pecuniary Benefits', *Journal of Human Resources* 11, 1976.

EHRLICH, I., 'On the Relationship between Education and Crime', in Juster, F. T. (ed.), *Education, Income and Human Behavior*. McGraw-Hill, New York, 1975.

El Pais, 'Los Pecados de la Iglesia, Edicion Internacional', 20 January 1997.

ESMAN, M. J., 'Political and Psychological Factors in Ethnic Conflict', in Montville, J. (ed.), *Conflict and Peacemaking in Multiethnic Societies*. Lexington Books, Lexinton MA and Toronto, 1990.

ESMAN, M. J., *Ethnic Politics*. Cornell University Press, Ithaca, 1994.

FANON, F., *The Wretched of the Earth*. Grove Press, New York, 1968, c1963.

FERGUSON, ROBERT, 'Children, Ethnic Conflict and the Media'. Unpublished background paper prepared for UNICEF International Child Development Centre, Florence, 1998.

FIRER, R., 'Ethnicity and Conflict: The Role of Education Project:The Case of Israel'. Unpublished background paper, UNICEF International Child Development Centre, Florence, 1998.

FOUNDATION ON INTER-ETHNIC RELATIONS, 'The Hague Recommendations Regarding the Education Rights of National Minorities and Explanatory Note'. Foundation on Inter-Ethnic Relations, The Hague, 1996.

GALLAGHER, A.M., 'Education Policy Approaches in Multi-Ethnic Societies'. Unpublished background paper prepared for UNICEF International Child Development Centre, Florence, 1998.

GINTIS, H., 'Education, Technology, and the Characteristics of Worker Productivity'. *American Economic Review*, 61, 1971.

GLAZER, N. and D. P. MOYNIHAN, *Ethnicity: Theory and Experience*. Harvard University Press, Cambridge MA, 1975.

GRAHAM-BROWN, S., *Education in the Developing World: Conflict and Crisis*. World University Service, London, 1991.

GRAHAM-BROWN, S., 'The Role of the Curriculum', in *Education Rights and Minorities* . Minority Rights Group, London, 1994.

GRANT, N. (ed.), Education and Minority Groups: Special Issue, *Comparative Education*, 24 (2), 1998.

GUNDARA, J., 'Ethnic Co-Existence, Conflict and Violence; the Role of Education'. Unpublished background paper prepared for UNICEF International Child Development Centre, Florence, 1998.

GURR T. R., *Minorities at Risk. A Global View of Ethnopolitical Conflicts*. United States Institute of Peace Press, Washington D.C., 1993.

HAHN, CAROLE L., *Comparative Perspectives on Citizenship: A Five Nation Study*. SUNY Press, Albany, 1997.

HAMMARBERG, T., 'A School for Children with Rights: the Significance of the United Nations Convention on the Rights of the Child for Modern Education Policy', *Innocenti Lecture*. UNICEF, International Child Development Centre, Florence, 1998.

HAVEMAN, R.H. and B. WOLFE, 'Schooling and Economic Well-Being: the Role of Nonmarket Effects', *Journal of Human Resources* 19 (Summer), 1984.

HEYNEMAN, S. P., 'Education in the Europe and Central Asia Region: Policies of Adjustment and Excellence', in F.J.H. Mertons (ed.) *Reflections on Education in Russia*. Amersfort, Acco, 1995a.

HEYNEMAN, S. P., *Thoughts on Social Stabilization*. CIVITAS, Prague 1995b.

HEYNEMAN, S. P., 'From the Party/State to Multi-Ethnic Democracy: Education and its Influence on Social Cohesion in the Europe and Central Asia Region'. Unpublished background paper prepared for UNICEF International Child Development Centre, Florence, 1998.

HEYNEMAN, S. P., 'Transition from Party/State to Open Democracy: the Role of Education', *International Journal of Education Development* 18, no. 1,1998.

HOBBES, T., *Leviathan*. Penguin Books, Harmondsworth, 1968.

HOROWITZ, D. L., *Ethnic Groups in Conflict*. University of Chicago Press, Chicago, 1987.

HOROWITZ, D. L., 'Ethnic Conflict Management for Policymakers', in Montville, J. (ed.), *Conflict and Peacemaking in Multiethnic Societies*. Lexington Books, Lexington MA and Toronto, 1990.

HOWE, K. R., 'In Defence of Outcomes-Based Conceptions of Equal Educational Opportunity'. *Educational Theory*, 39 (4), 1989.

HYMAN, HERBERT H. and CHARLES R. WRIGHT, *Education's Lasting Influence on Values*. Chicago, University of Chicago Press, 1979.

INKELES, A. and D. H. SMITH, *Becoming Modern*. Harvard University Press, Cambridge MA, 1974.

KAMIN, L. J., *The Science and Politics of IQ*. Penguin, London, 1977.

KAMENS, DAVID, 'Education and Democracy: a Comparative Institutional Analysis', *Sociology of Education* 61,1998.

KIDRON, M. and R. SEGAL, *The New State of the World Atlas*. London, Pluto Press, 1984.

KOHN, M., *The Race Gallery*. London, Jonathan Cape, 1995.

KYMLICKA, W., *The Rights of Minority Cultures*. Oxford University Press, Oxford, 1996.

LE VINE, VICTOR T., and CAMPBELL, 1972, n.a.

LINDEN, I., *Church and Revolution in Rwanda*. Manchester University Press, Manchester, 1977.

MARTINEZ, K, 'Problems of Ehnic and Cultural Differences between Teachers and Students: a Story of a Beginning Teacher of Australian Aboriginal Children', *Journal of Education for Teaching*, 20 (2), 1994.

McDOWALL, D., *The Kurds*. Minority Rights Group, London, 1996.

MENNONITE CENTRAL COMMITTEE OF CANADA (MCCC), 'Submission of MCCC to the Canadian Council for International Cooperation (CCIC) Foreign Policy Review: A Framework for Our Common Future', prepared by Chris Derksen Hiebert and Joanne Epp. Mennonite Central Committee of Canada, Ottawa, 1993.

MEYER, J. W., 'The Charter: Conditions of Diffuse Socialization in Schools', in W.R. Scott (ed.), *Social Processes and Social Structure*. Holt Rinehart and Winston, New York, 1970.

MODGIL, S., G.K. VERMA, K. MALLICK, and C. MODGIL (eds.), *Multicultural Education, the Interminable Debate*. Falmer Press, London, 1986.

MONTVILLE, J. (ed.), *Conflict and Peacemaking in Multiethnic Societies*. Lexington Books, Lexington MA and Toronto, 1990.

NEWBURY, C., *The Cohesion of Oppression: Clientship and Ethnicity in Rwanda (1860-1960)*. Columbia University Press, New York, 1988.

NIE, N.H., J. JUNN, and B.K. STEHLIK, *Education and Democratic Citizenship in America*. University of Chicago Press, Chicago, 1996.

NIEMI, R., and M. HEPBURN, 'The Rebirth of Political Socialization'. *Perspectives on Political Science* 24,1995.

NISSAN, E., *Sri Lanka: A Bitter Harvest*. Minority Rights Group, London, 1996.

NORDSTROM, C. and J. MARTIN (eds.), *The Paths to Domination, Resistance and Terror*. University of California Press, Berkeley and London, 1992.

OLSON, M., 'The Treatment of Externalities in.National Income Statistics', in Lowdon Wingo and Alan Evans (eds.), *Public Economics and the Quality of Life*. John Hopkins University Press, Baltimore, 1977.

OLSON, M. and R. ZECKHAUSER, 'The Priority of Public Problems', in Marris, R. (ed.), *The Corporate Society*. London, Macmillan, 1974.

OMAAR, RAKIY, 'Somaliland: One Thorn at a Time', *Current History*, May, 1994.

PADILLA, A.M. and R.A. RUIZ, *Latino Mental Health: a Review of the Literature*. National Institute of Mental Health, Rockville, Md. 1974.

PARKIN, F., 'Social Stratification', in Bottomore, T. and R. Nisbet (eds), *A History of Sociological Analysis*. Heinemann Educational Books, London, 1979.

POSTMAN, N., *The End of Education: Redefining the Value of School*. Vintage Books, New York, 1996.

POULTON, H., *The Balkans: Minorities and States in Conflict*. London, Minority Rights Group, 1991.

PROJECT ON ETHNIC RELATIONS, 'Managing Ethnic Conflict: The Kona Statement. Princeton, New Jersey , April 1994. Found at http://pwl.netcom.com/~ethnie/kona1.html, October 1998.

PURYEAR, J. M., *Thinking Politics: Intellectuals and Democracy in Chile 1973-1988*. Baltimore, Johns Hopkins University Press, 1994.

REEVES, P., 'Best of Enemies Rewrite History of Hate'. *The Independent*, 4 October 1998.

REX, J., *Race and Ethnicity*. Open University Press, Welwyn Garden City, 1986.

RICHARDS, E., 'The Debate about Peace Education', *Background Paper # 10*. Canadian Institute for International Peace and Security, December 1986.

RIEGEL, KLAUS F. and JOHN A. MEACHAM (eds), *The Developing Individual in a Changing World*. The Hague, Mouton, 1976.

RULE, J., *Theories of Civil Violence*. University of Califomia Press, Berkeley and Los Angeles, 1988.

SAUNDERS, J., *Academic Freedom in Indonesia: Dismantling Soeherto-Era Barriers*. Human Rights Watch, New York, 1998.

SCARRY, E., *The Body in Pain: The Making and Unmaking of the World*. Oxford University Press, New York, 1985.

SELLSTROM, T. and L. WOHLGEMUTH, 'The International Response to Conflict and Genocide: Lessons from the Rwanda Experience. Historical Perspective: Some Explanatory Factors'. Joint Evaluation of Emergency Assistance to Rwanda, *Journal of Humanitarian Assistance*, 1996.

SEMENIUK, R., 'War Babies, the Children of the Gaza Strip', *Equinox Magazine*, Camden East, January/February 1995.

STOCKHOLM INTERNATIONAL PEACE RESEARCH INSTITUTE, *SIPRI Yearbook 1998: Armaments, Disarmament and International Security*. Oxford University Press, Oxford, 1998.

STAUB, E., *The Roots of Evil: The Origins of Genocide and Other Group Violence*. Cambridge University Press, Cambridge, 1989.

STAVENHAGEN, R., *Ethnic Conflicts and the Nation-State*. Macmillan Press Ltd., 1996.

STAVENHAGEN, R., 'Double Jeopardy: The Children of Ethnic Minonities', *Innocenti Occasional Paper*, CRS 10. UNICEF International Child Developemnt Centre, 1994.

STAVENHAGEN, R., *The Ethnic Question*. Japan: United Nations University, 1991.

STREMLAU, J., *People in Peril, Human Rights, Humanitarian Action, and Preventing Deadly Conflict*. Carnegie Corporation of New York, New York,1998.

TAJFEL, H. (ed), 'The Social Dimension: European Developments', in *Social Psychology*, Vol. 2. Cambridge University Press, Cambridge, 1984.

TARROW, N.B. (ed), *Human Rights and Education*. Pergamon Press, London, 1987.

TORNEY-PURTA, JUDITH V., 'Links and Missing Links Between Education, Political Knowledge and Citizenship', *American Journal of Education*, August, 1997.

TORNEY-PURTA, JUDITH V., 'The Second IEA Civics Education Project: Development of Content Guidelines and Items for a Cross-National Test and Survey', *Canadian and International Education* 25, 1996.

TORNEY-PURTA, JUDITH V., 'Psychological Theory as a Basis for Political Socialization Research', *Perspectives on Political Science*, 24, 1994.

TORNEY-PURTA, JUDITH V., ABRAHAM N. OPPENHEIM, and RUSSELL FARNEN, *Civic Education in Ten Countries: An Ernpirical Study.* New York, Halsted, 1975.

TORNEY-PURTA, JUDITH V. and John Schwille, 'Civic Values Learned in School: Policy and Practice in Industrialized Nations', *Comparative Education Review* 30, no. 1, 1986.

UNITED NATIONS CHILDREN'S FUND, *Education and Change in Central and Eastern Europe*, Report of the Education for Development Seminar. UNICEF, Bulgaria, 1993.

UNITED NATIONS CHILDREN'S FUND, *Emergency Operations in Former Yugoslavia.* UNICEF Belgrade, 1994.

UNITED NATIONS CHILDREN'S FUND, 'Children of Minorities: Deprivation and Discrimination', *Innocen ti Insight.* UNICEF International Child Development Centre, Florence, 1995.

UNITED NATIONS CHILDRENS FUND, *Federal Republic of Yugoslavia, Situation Analysis of Women and Children.* UNICEF Belgrade, 1996.

UNITED NATIONS CHILDREN'S FUND, *The State of the World's Children 1996.* Oxford University Press, New York, 1996.

UNITED NATIONS CHILDREN'S FUND, *Education for All?* MONEE Project Regional Monitoring Report. UNICEF International Child Development Centre, Florence, 1998.

UNITED NATIONS CHILDREN'S FUND, *The State of the World's Children 1999.* Oxford University Press, New York, 1999.

UNITED NATIONS CHILDREN'S FUND, 'The Kosovo Crisis: Humanitarian Assistance In Albania, The Federal Republic Of. Yugoslavia, Fyr Macedonia, and Bosnia and Herzegovina, April-June 1999'. A working document based on information available 6 April 1999.

UNITED NATIONS ECONOMIC AND SOCIAL COUNCIL, COMMISSION ON HUMAN RIGHTS, 'The Impact of Armed Conflict on Children: Report of the Expert of the Secretary General, Ms Graça Machel', UN Document A/51/306, 26 August 1996a.

UNITED NATIONS ECONOMIC AND SOCIAL COUNCIL, COMMISSION ON HUMAN RIGHTS, 'Situation of Human Rights in the Territory of the Former Yugoslavia. Special Report on Minorities', Periodic report submitted by Ms. Elisabeth Rehn, Special Rapporteur of the Commission on Human Rights, pursuant to paragraph 45 of Commission Resolution 1996/71, E/CN.4/1997/8, 25 October 1996b.

UNITED NATIONS ECONOMIC AND SOCIAL COUNCIL, COMMITTEE ON THE RIGHTS OF THE CHILD, 'Concluding Observations of the Committee on the Rights of the Child: Croatia', CRC/C/15/Add.52,13 February1996c.

UNITED NATIONS ECONOMIC AND SOCIAL COUNCIL, SUB-COMMISSION ON PREVENTION OF DISCRIMINATION AND PROTECTION OF MINORITIES, 'Report of the Working Group on Minorities on its Third Session', E/CN.4/Sub.2/1997/18, 10 July 1997.

UNESCO, 'From War to Peace in History Books', in *UNESCO Education News*, No. 11, December 1997 - February 1998. UNESCO, Paris, 1998.

UPHOFF, N. T., 'Monitoring and Evaluating Popular Participation in World Bank-Assisted Projects', in Bhuvan Bhatnagar and Aubrey C. Williams (eds), *Participatory Development and the World Bank: Potential Directions for Change*, World Bank Discussion Paper No. 183. Washington, World Bank, 1992.

VERBA, SIDNEY, NORMAN NIE, and JAE-ON KIM, *Participation and Political Equality: A Seven Nation Comparison*. Cambridge University Press, Cambridge, 1978.

VIDYA BHARATI, Core Curriculum. Delhi, 1992. See www.vidyabharati.org

WACHTEL, P., 'The Effect of School Quality on Achievement, Attainment Levels, and Lifetime Earnings'. *Explorations in Economic Research* 2, 1975.

WOLFE, BARBARA and A. ZUVEKAS, A. *Non-Market Outcomes of Schooling*, Madison Wisconsin, Institute for Research on Poverty, May, 1997 (mimeograph).

WOLFENSON, J., New Directions and New Partnerships: Address to the Board of Governors, 10 October 1995. Full text available from the World Bank website http://jolis.worldbankimflib.org/external.htm

WORLD VISION INTERNATIONAL, *The Effects of Armed Conflicts on Girls*. World Vision, Geneva, 1996.

YOSSI, S., 'Segregation, Tracking, and the Educational Attainment of Minorities: Arabs and Oriental Jews in Israel', *American Sociological Review*, vol. 55, no. 1, 1990.